Atlas Of Human Anatomy:

Kids Guide Book

ISBN: 978-1-6814-5999-8

First Printed 03/19/2015

Circulatory System

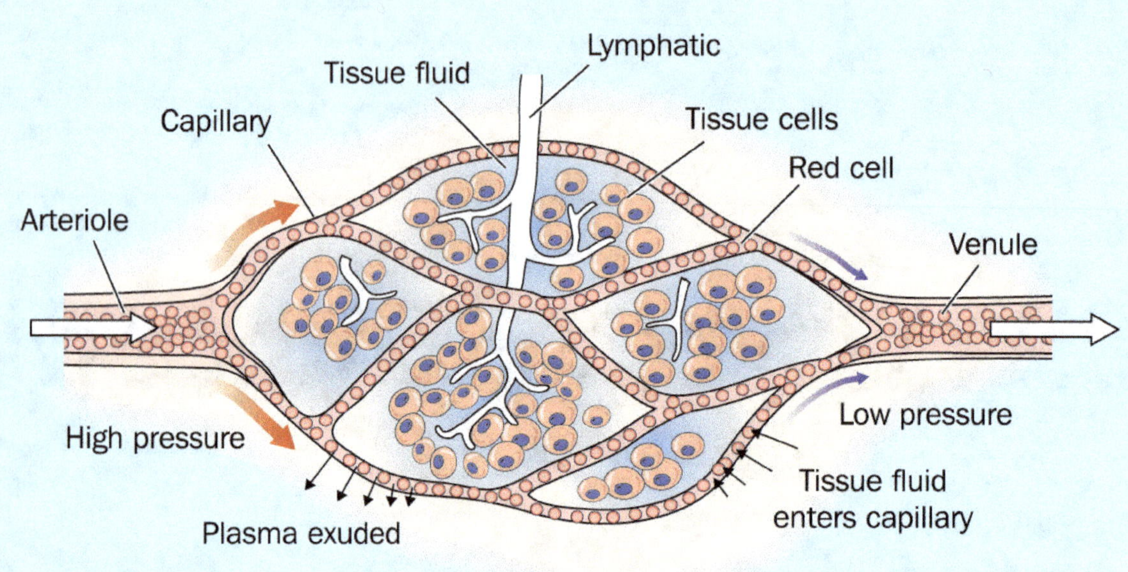

Capillary bed

Circulatory System Capilary Blood Flow

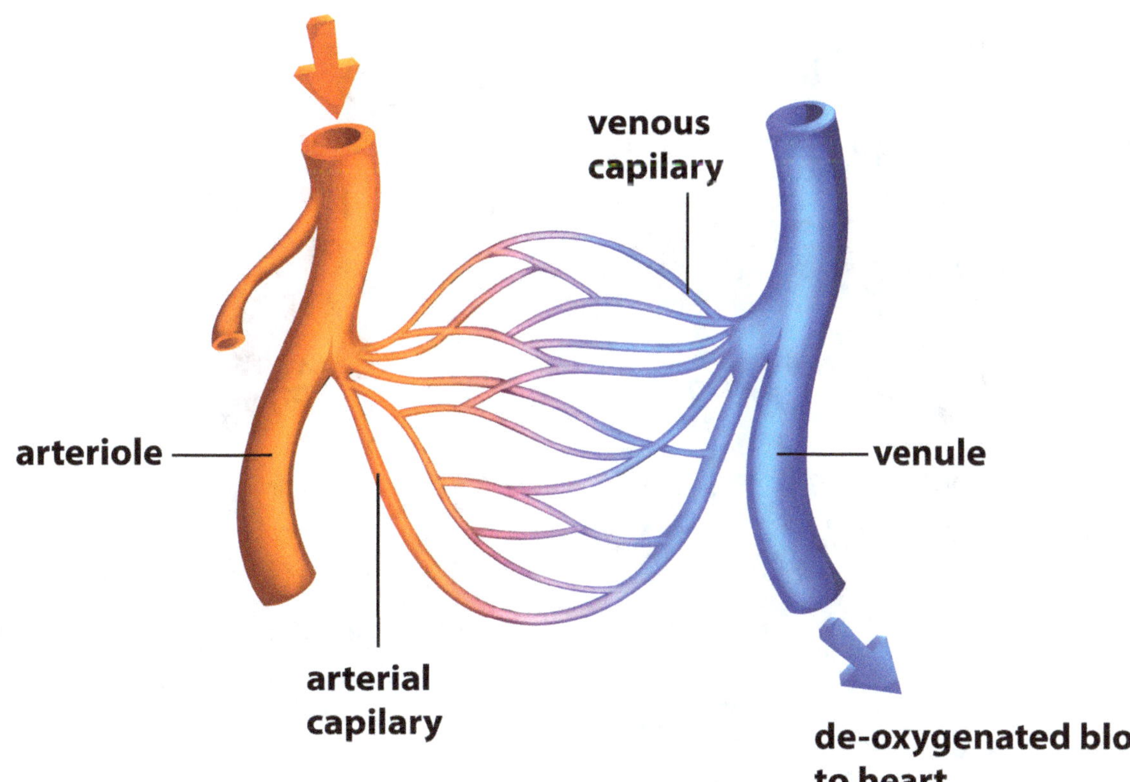

CIRCULATORY

Blood Flow in Human Circulatory System

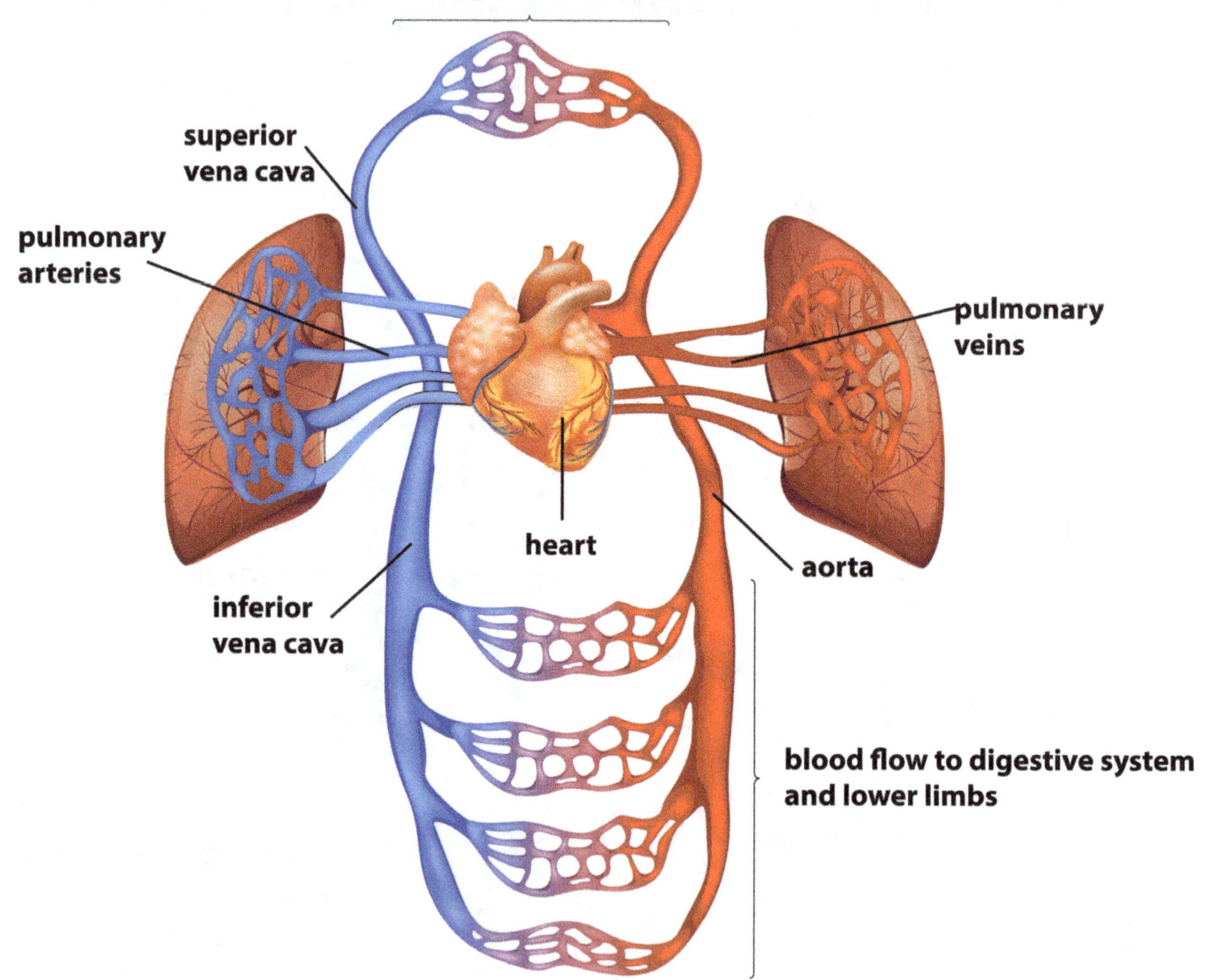

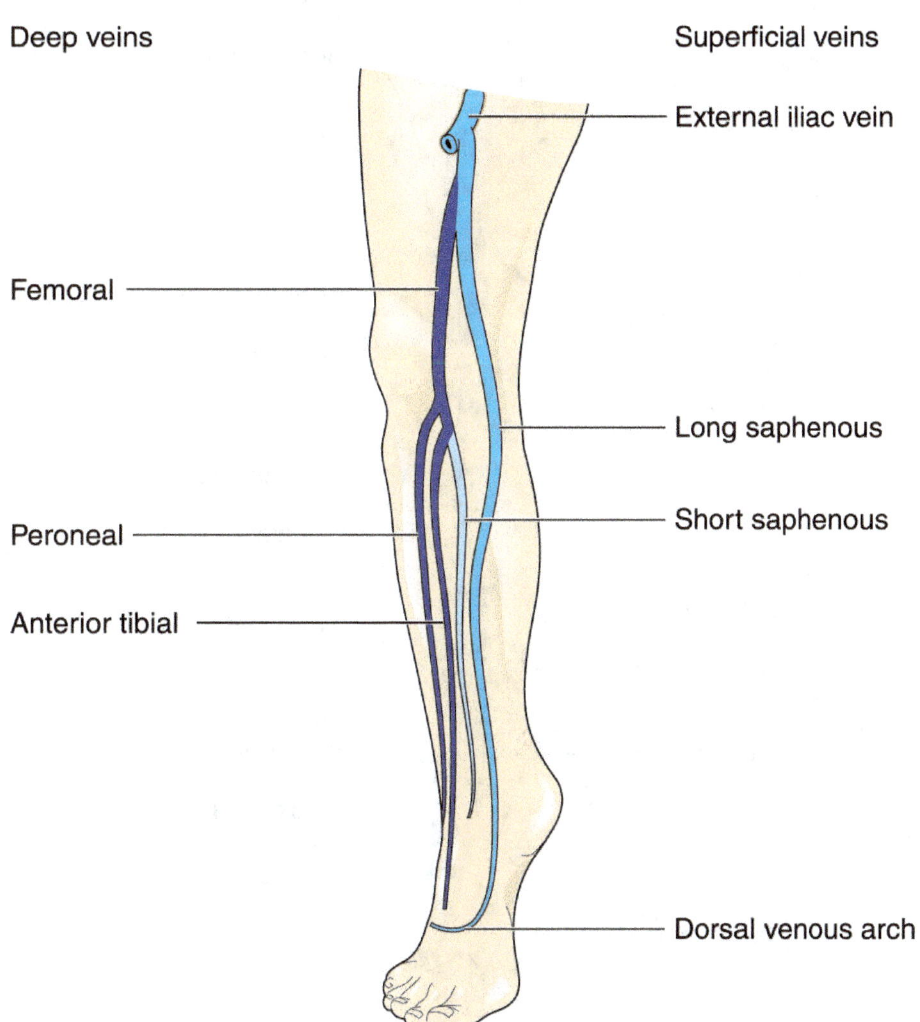
Deep veins
Superficial veins
External iliac vein
Femoral
Long saphenous
Short saphenous
Peroneal
Anterior tibial
Dorsal venous arch

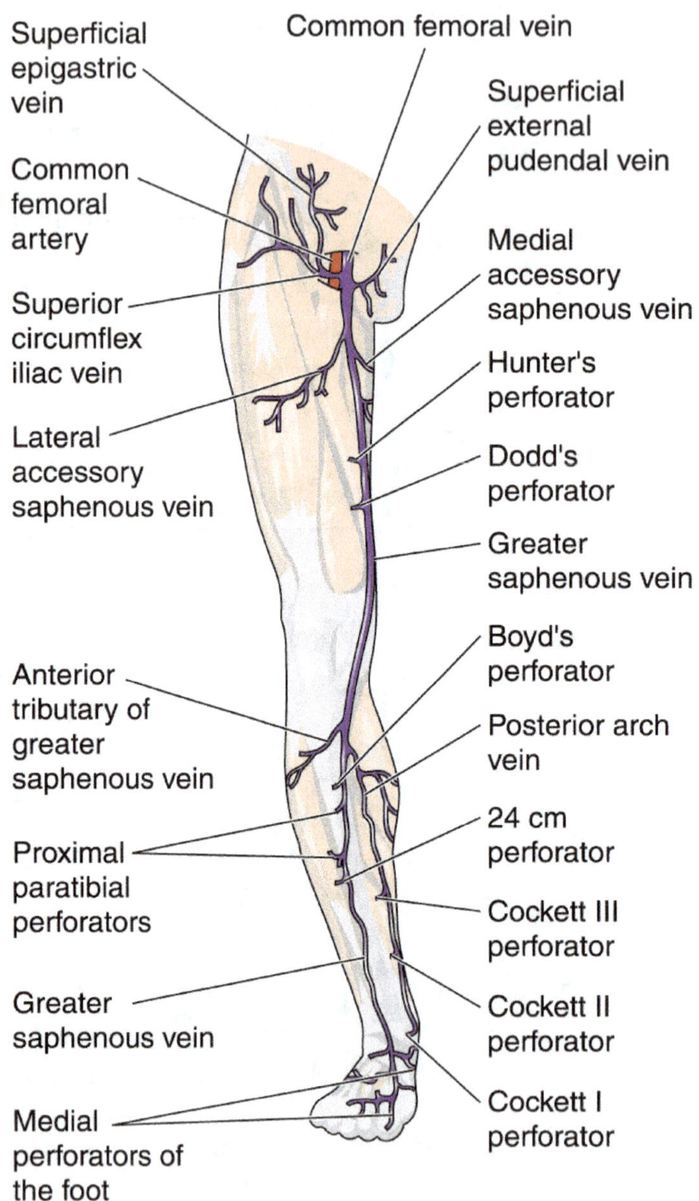
Superficial epigastric vein
Common femoral vein
Superficial external pudendal vein
Common femoral artery
Medial accessory saphenous vein
Superior circumflex iliac vein
Hunter's perforator
Lateral accessory saphenous vein
Dodd's perforator
Greater saphenous vein
Boyd's perforator
Anterior tributary of greater saphenous vein
Posterior arch vein
24 cm perforator
Proximal paratibial perforators
Cockett III perforator
Greater saphenous vein
Cockett II perforator
Medial perforators of the foot
Cockett I perforator

Digestive System

DIGESTIVE

Liver
Liver
Hepatic ducts
Stomach
Gall bladder
Cystic duct
Common bile duct
Pancreas
Duodenum

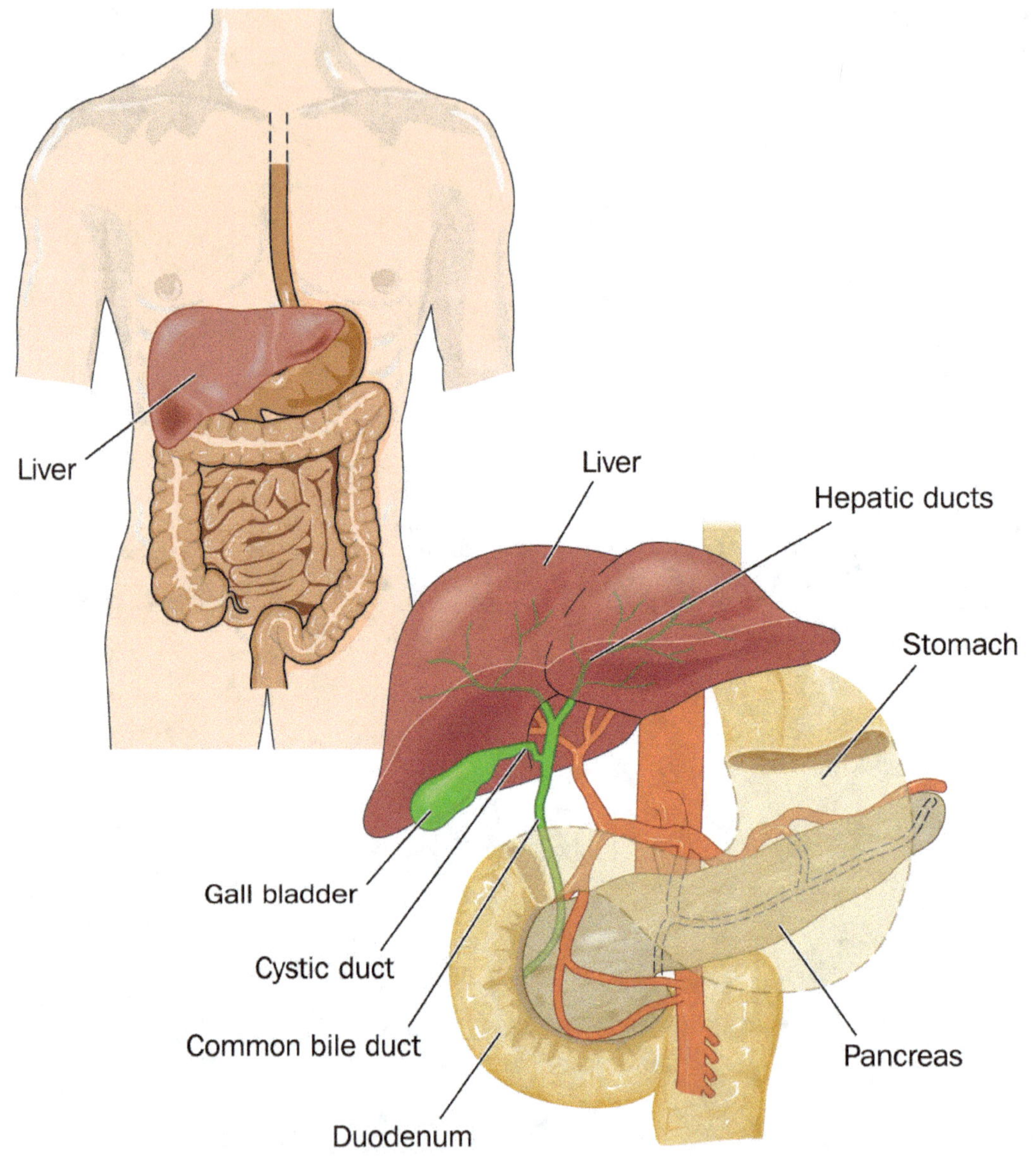

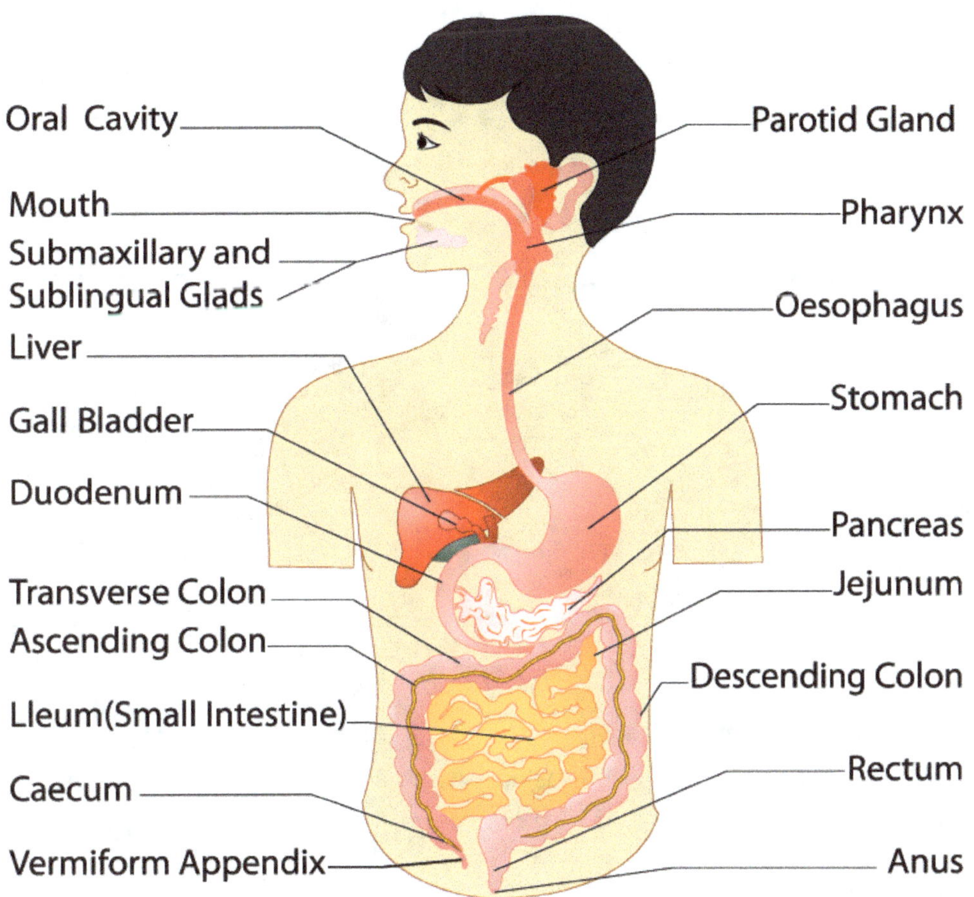
Oral Cavity
Mouth
Submaxillary and
Sublingual Glads
Liver
Gall Bladder
Duodenum
Transverse Colon
Ascending Colon
Lleum(Small Intestine)
Caecum
Vermiform Appendix
Parotid Gland
Pharynx
Oesophagus
Stomach
Pancreas
Jejunum
Descending Colon
Rectum
Anus

DIGESTIVE

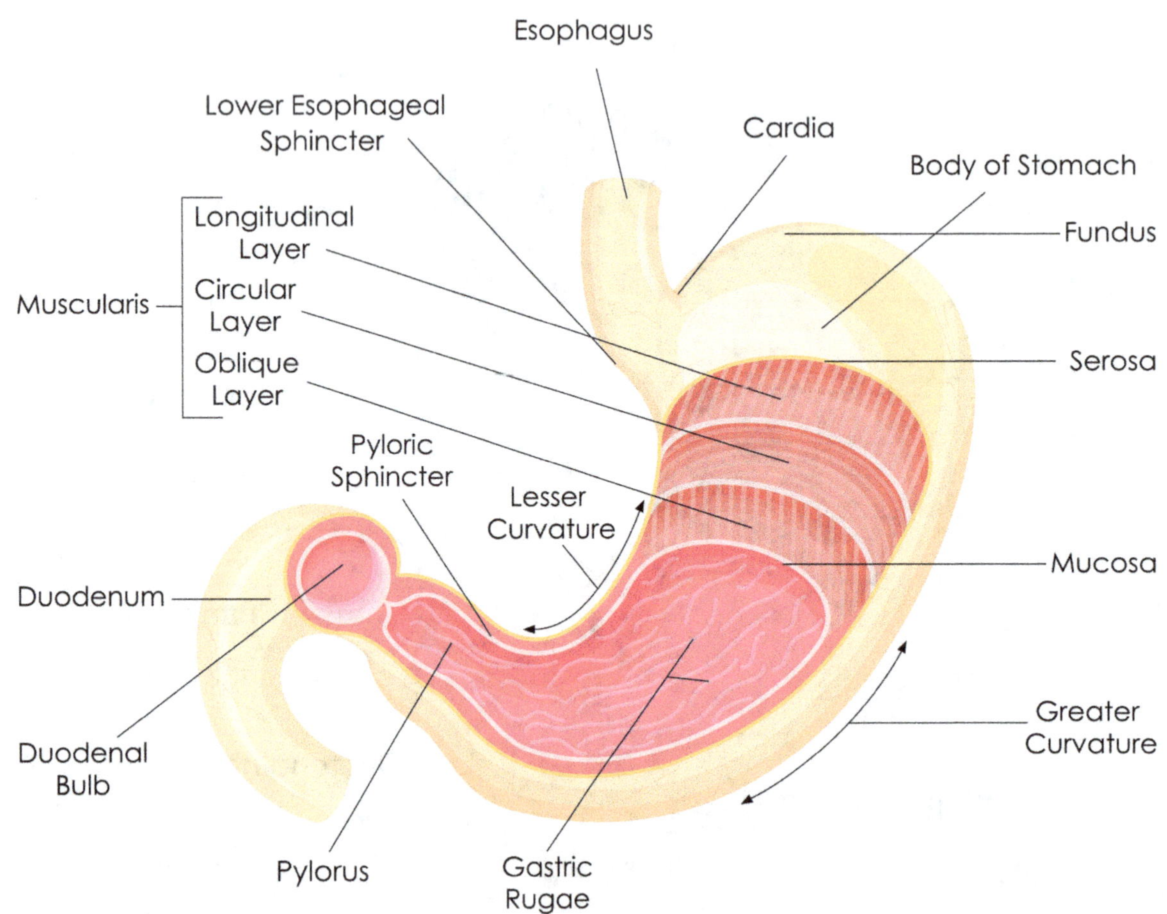

Stomach

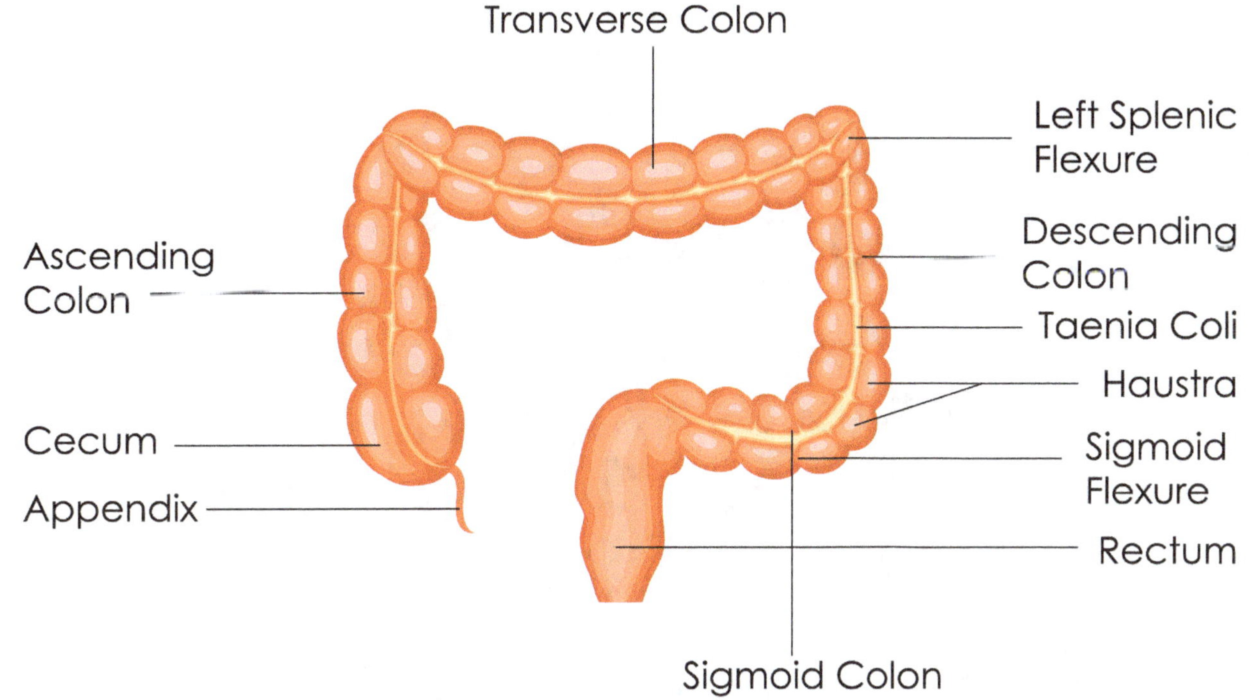

LARGE INTESTINE

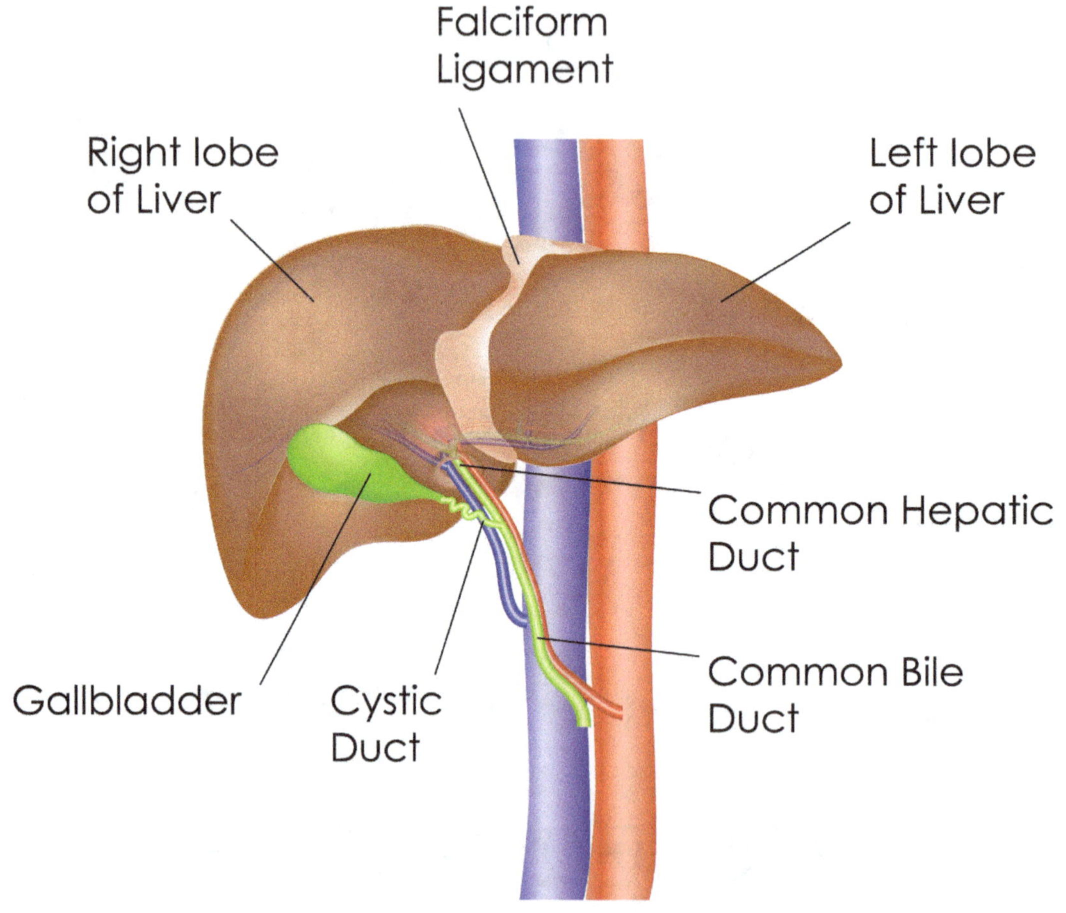
Falciform
Ligament
Right lobe
of Liver
Left lobe
of Liver
Common Hepatic
Duct
Common Bile
Duct
Gallbladder
Cystic
Duct

Endocrine System

Thyroid gland

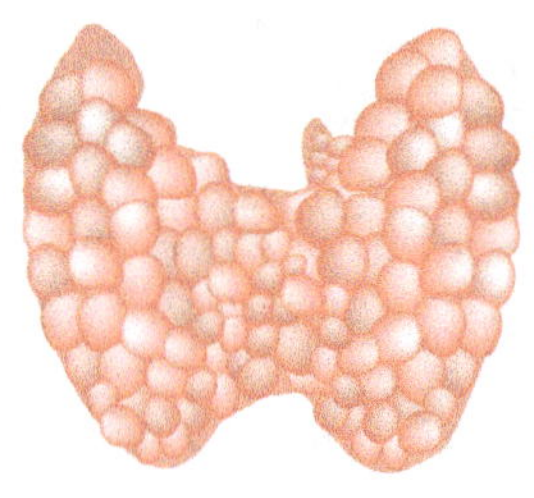

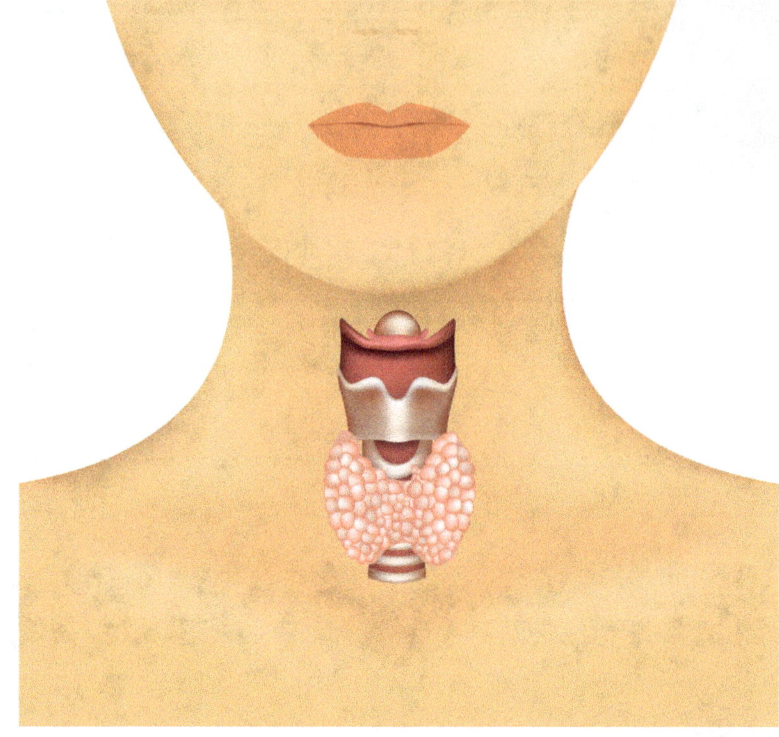

Thyroid Cartilage

Anterior

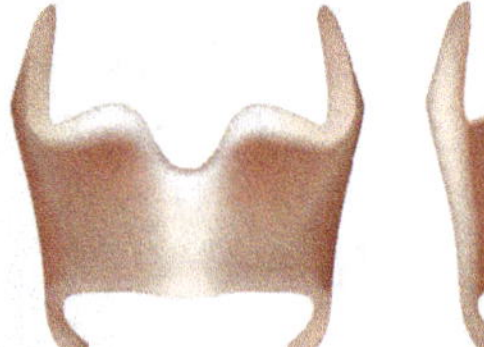

Posterior

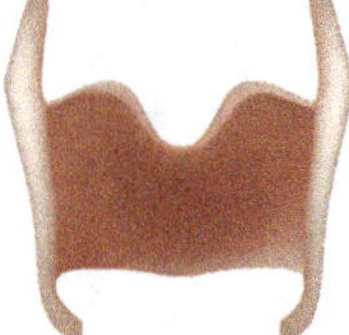

Anterior

Posterior

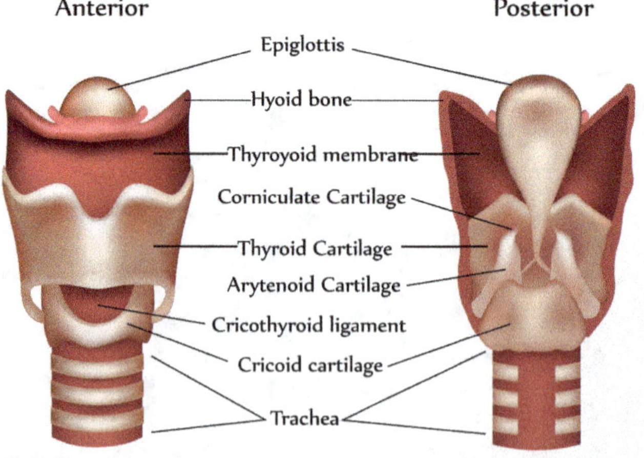

The Endocrine System

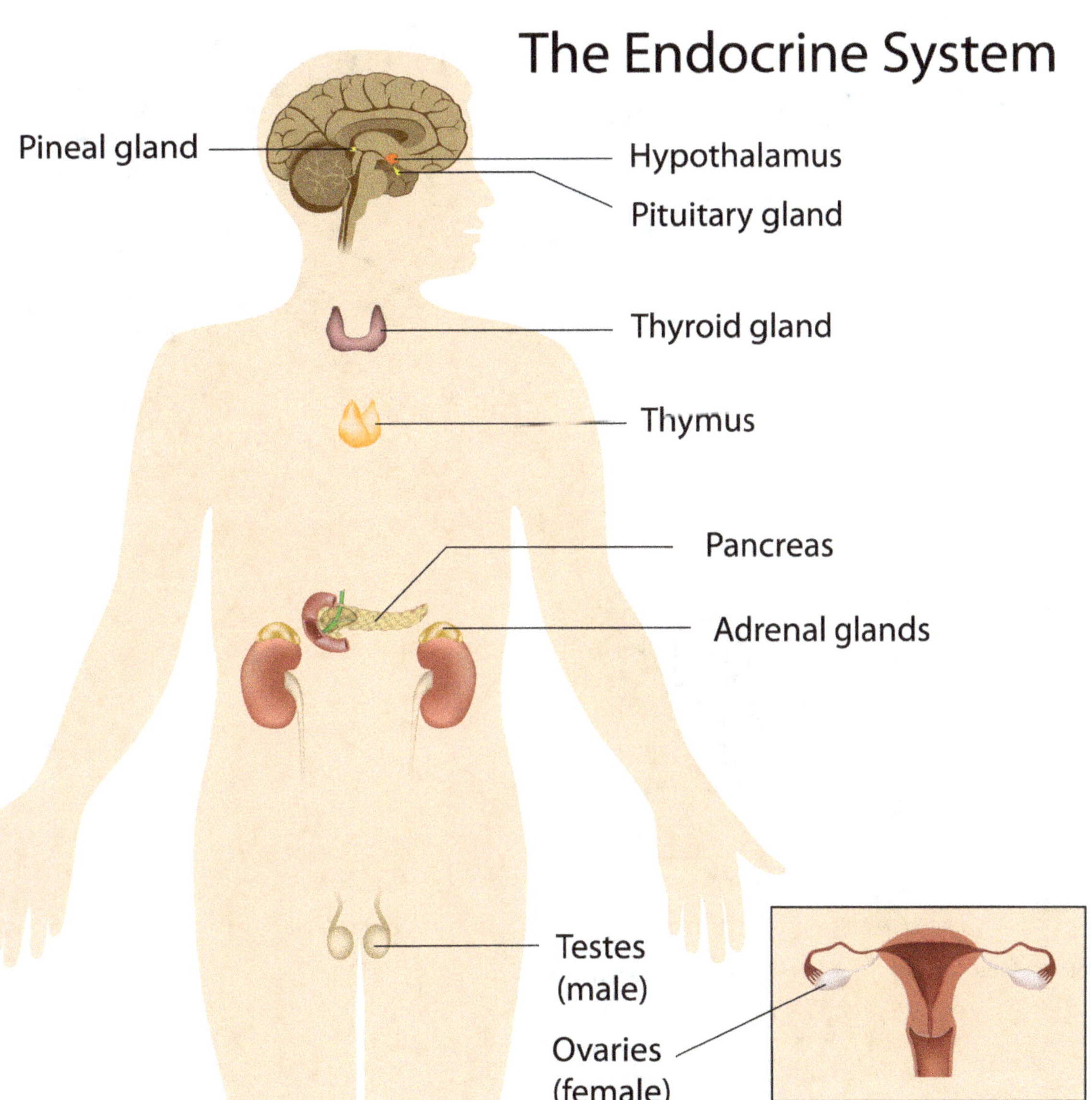

The Pituitary Gland

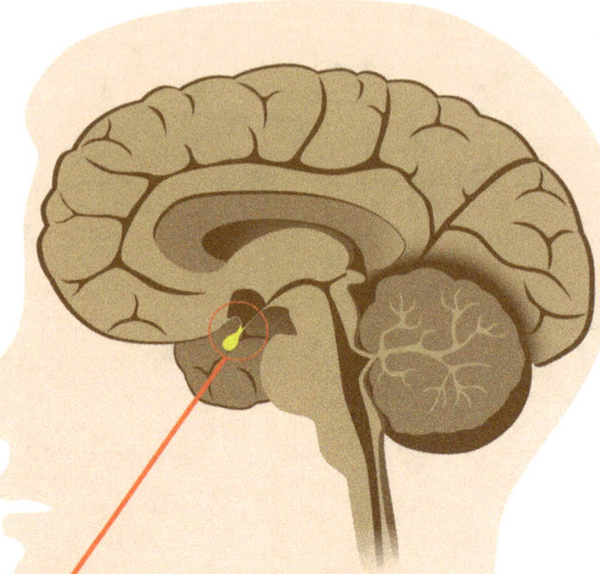

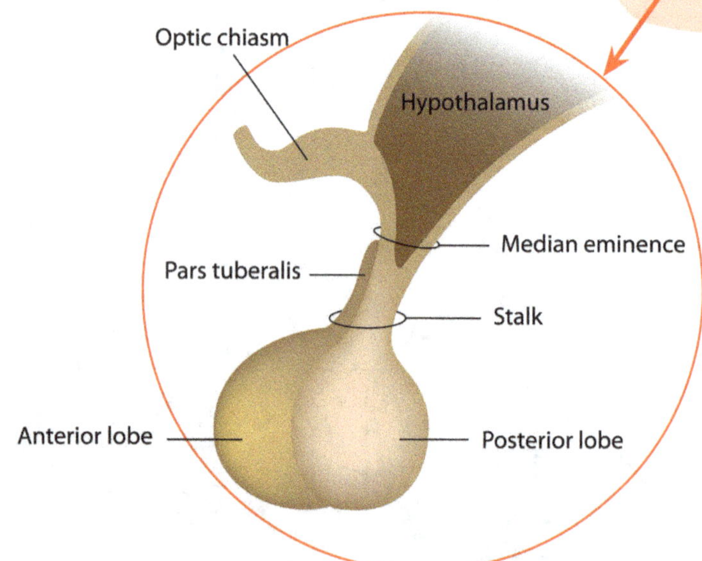

Endocrine gland

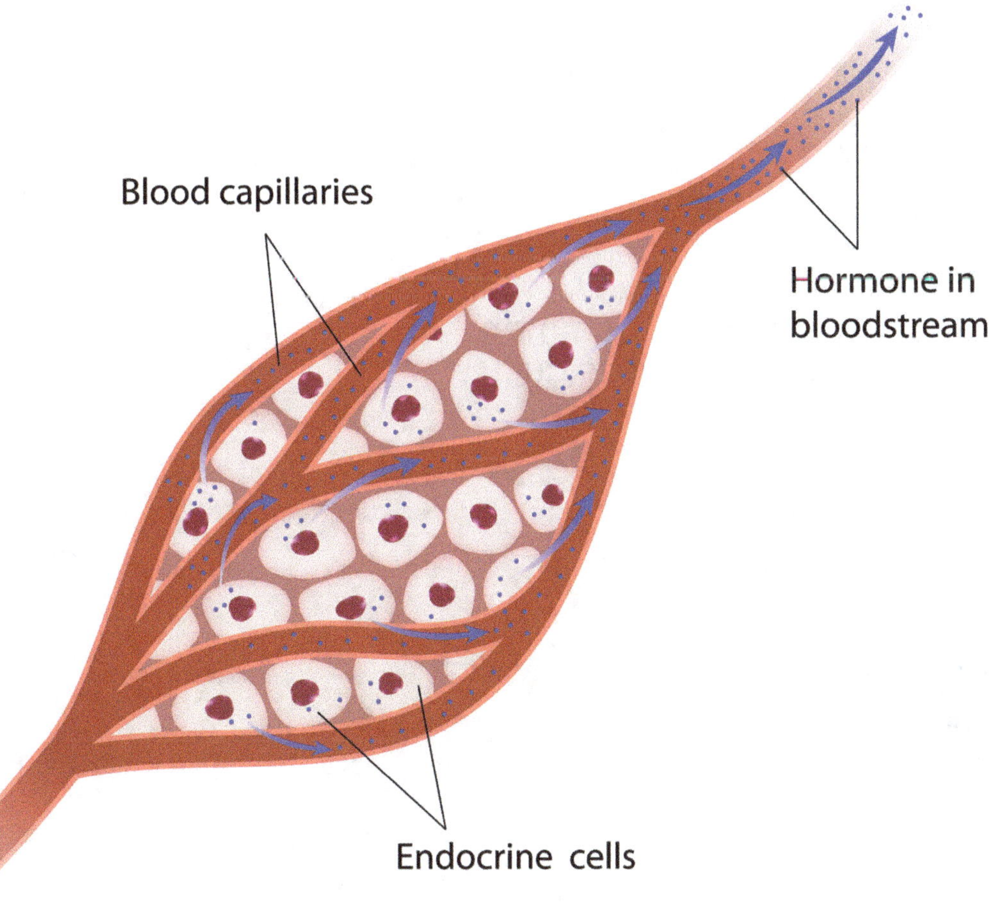

ENDOCRINE

PANCREAS

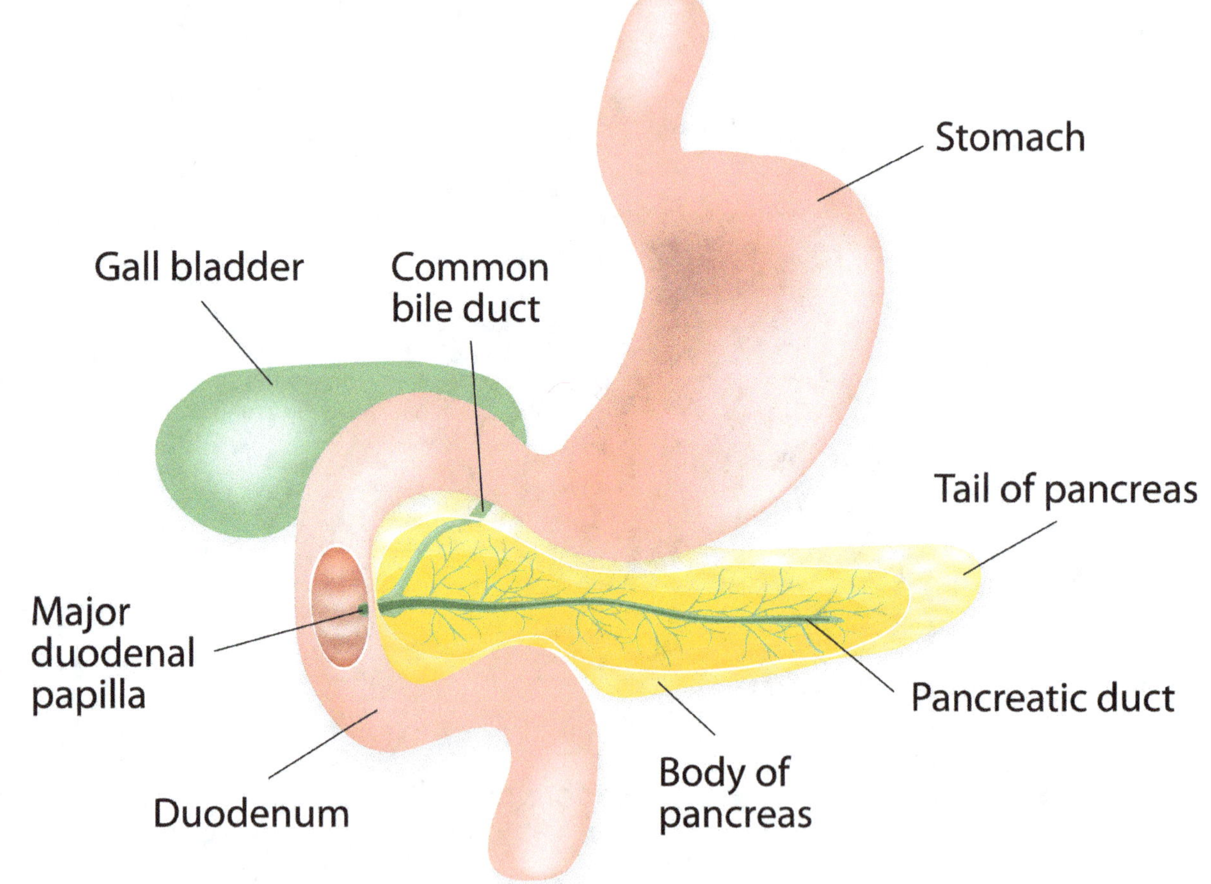

Lymphatic System

LYMPHATIC

The Lymphatic System

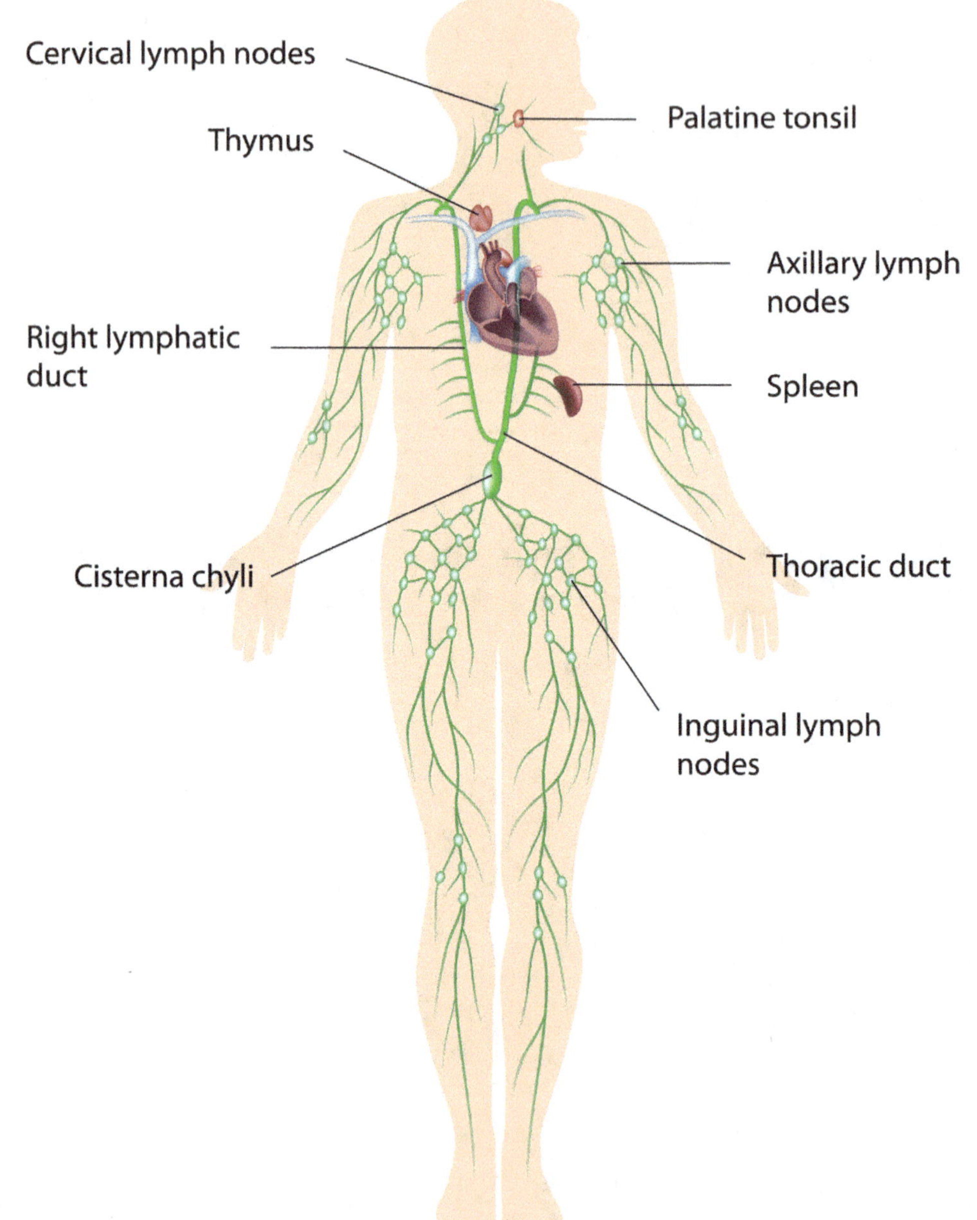

Anatomy of a Lymph Node

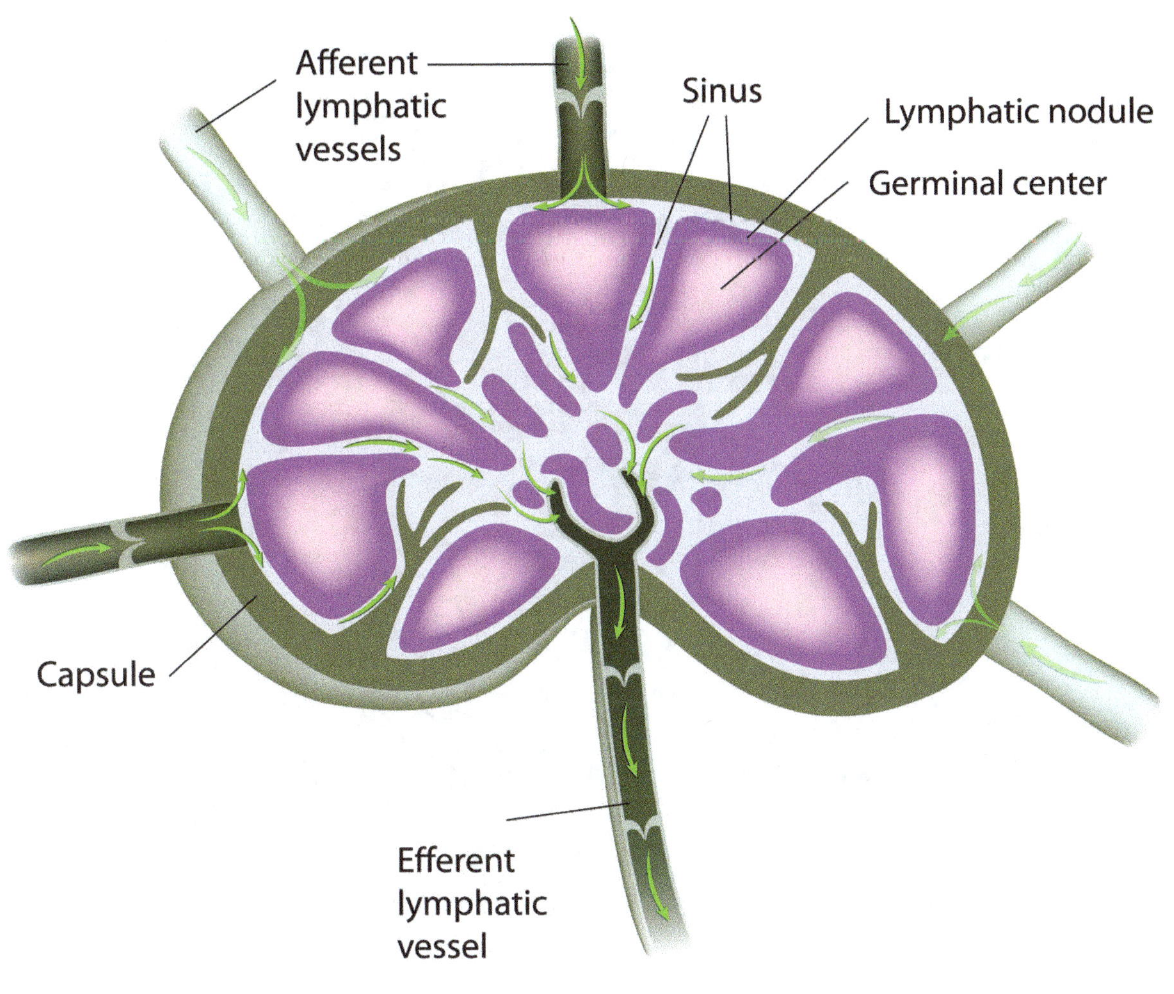

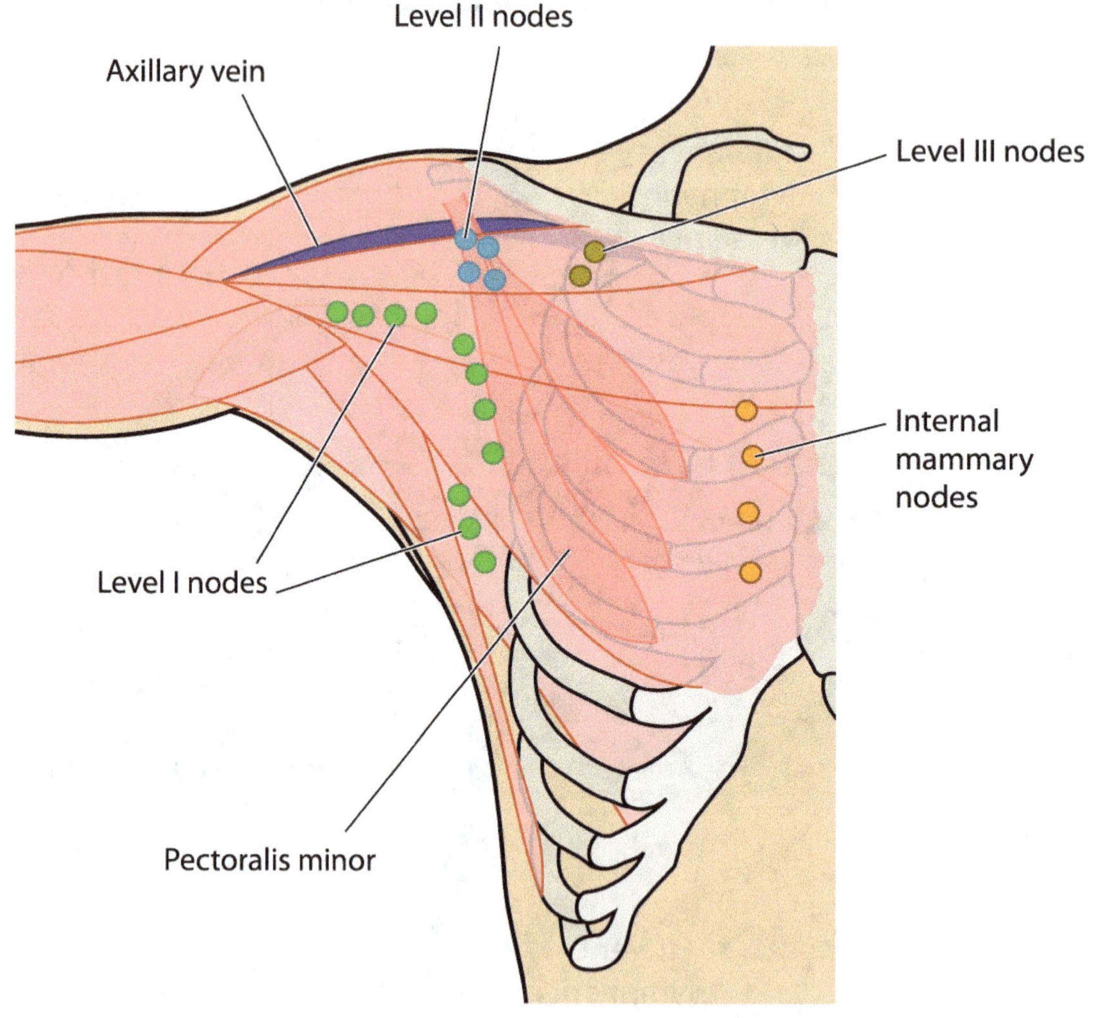
Level II nodes
Axillary vein
Level III nodes
Internal mammary nodes
Level I nodes
Pectoralis minor

Lymph Nodes of the Head and Neck

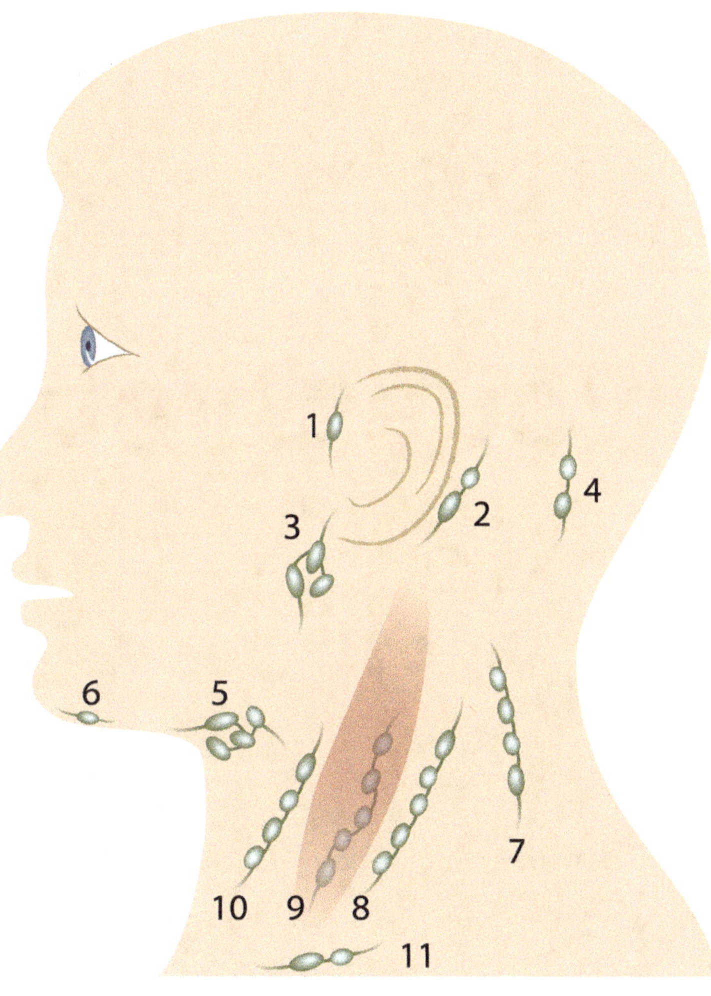

Nervous System

Anatomy of a Nerve

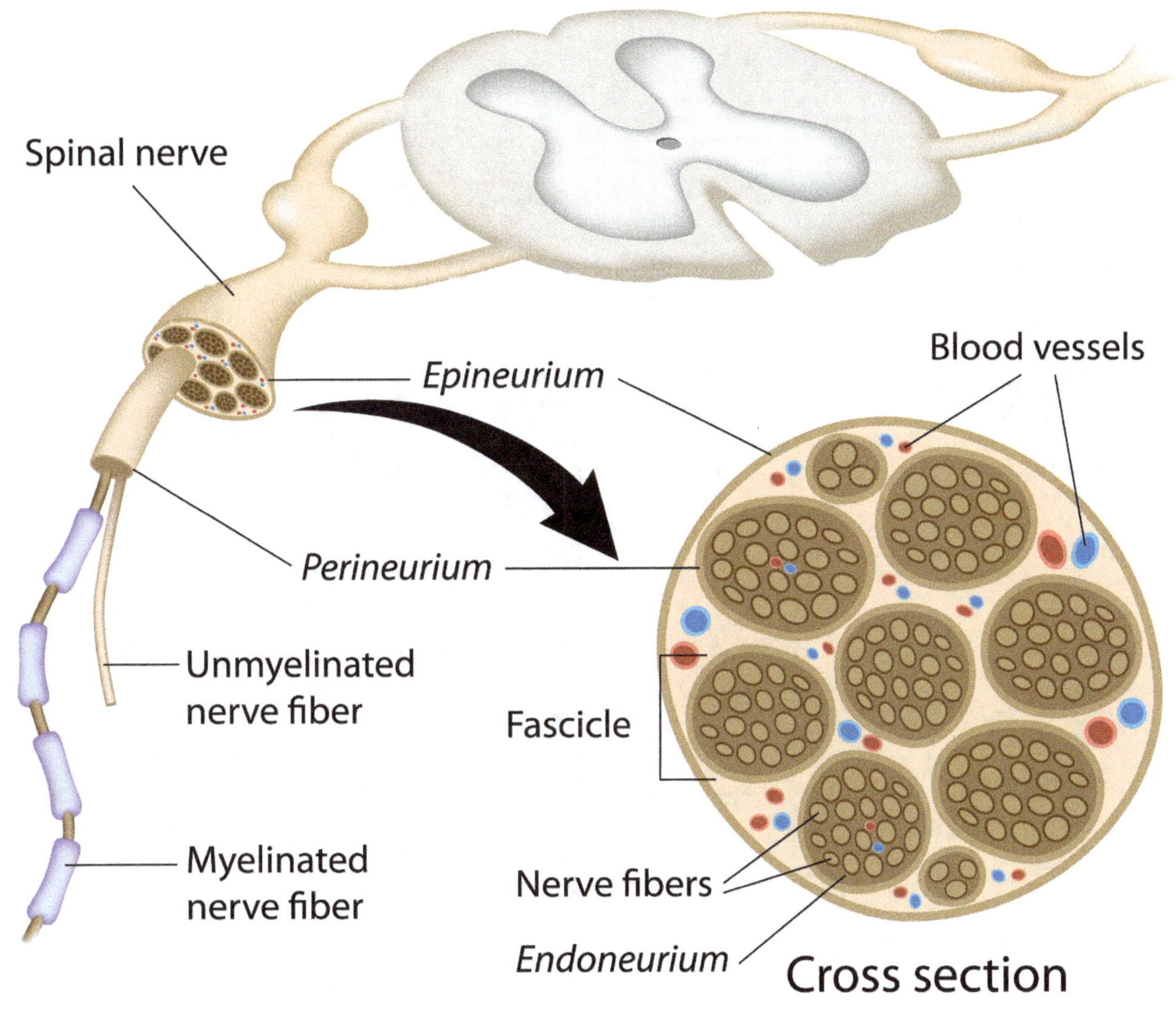

NERVOUS

The Lumbar Plexus

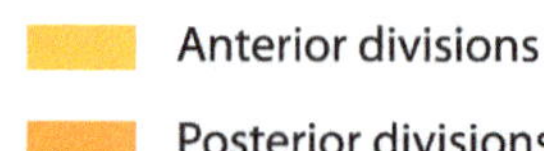

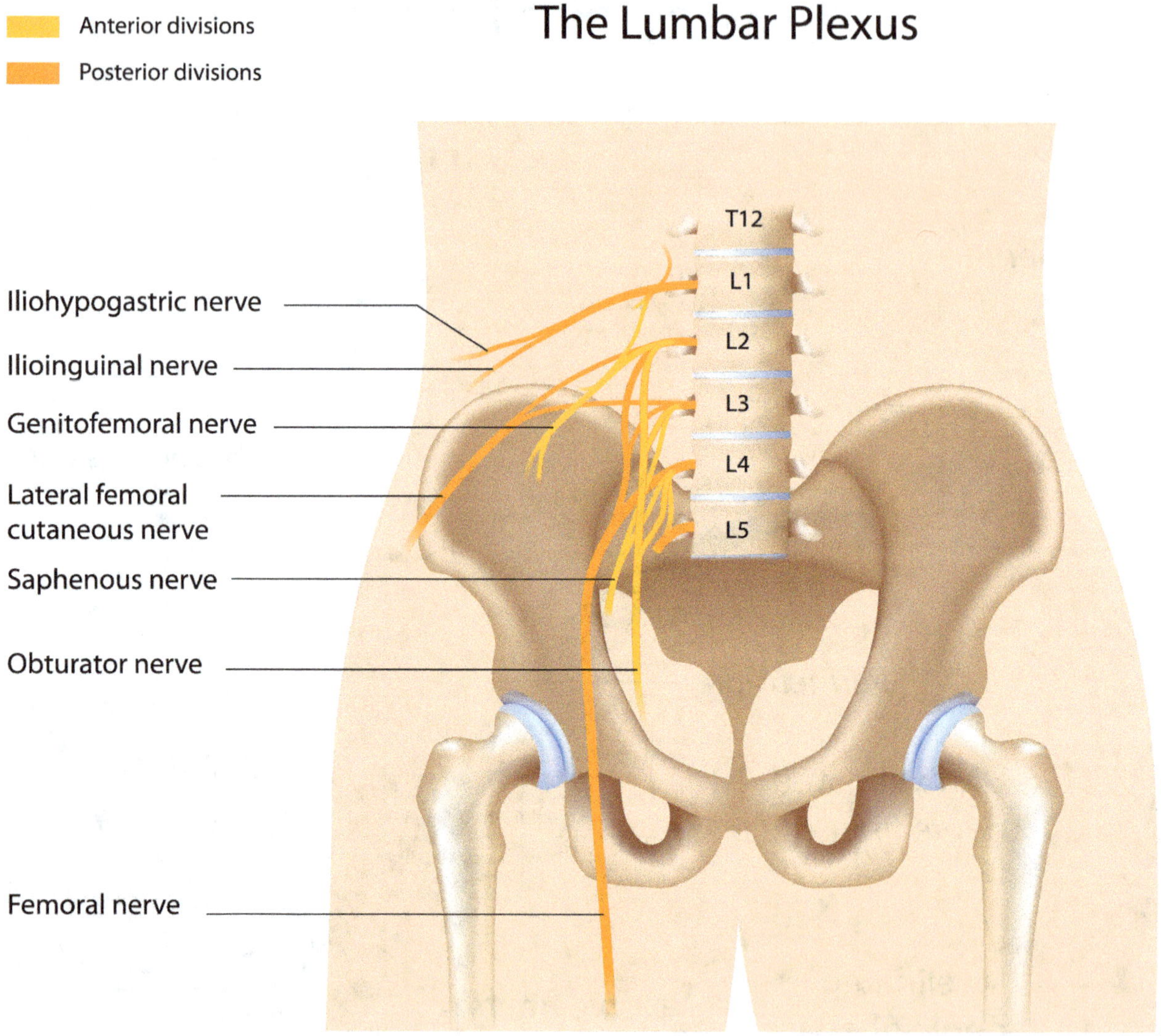

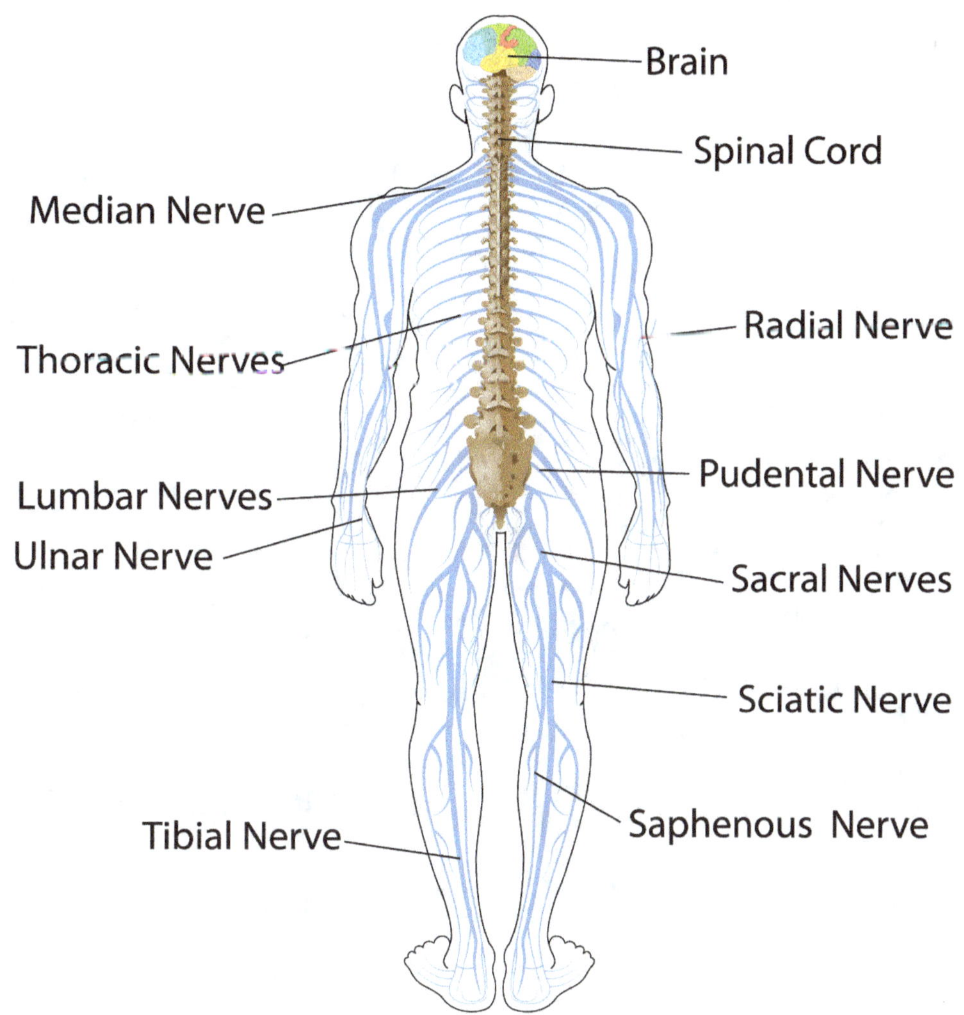
Brain
Spinal Cord
Median Nerve
Radial Nerve
Thoracic Nerves
Pudental Nerve
Lumbar Nerves
Ulnar Nerve
Sacral Nerves
Sciatic Nerve
Tibial Nerve
Saphenous Nerve

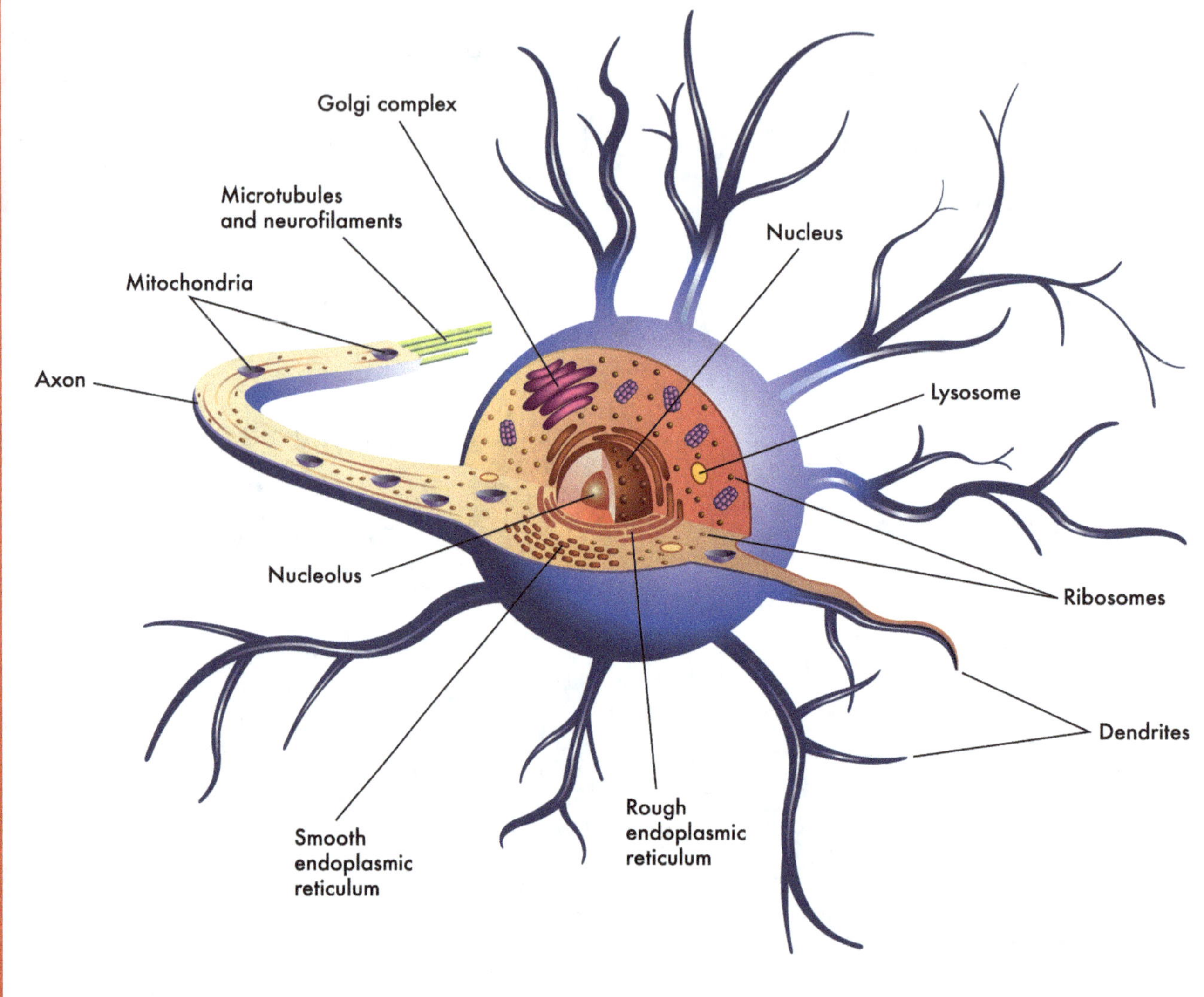
Golgi complex
Microtubules and neurofilaments
Mitochondria
Axon
Nucleus
Lysosome
Nucleolus
Ribosomes
Dendrites
Smooth endoplasmic reticulum
Rough endoplasmic reticulum

A multipolar neuron (Ex. spinal motor neuron)

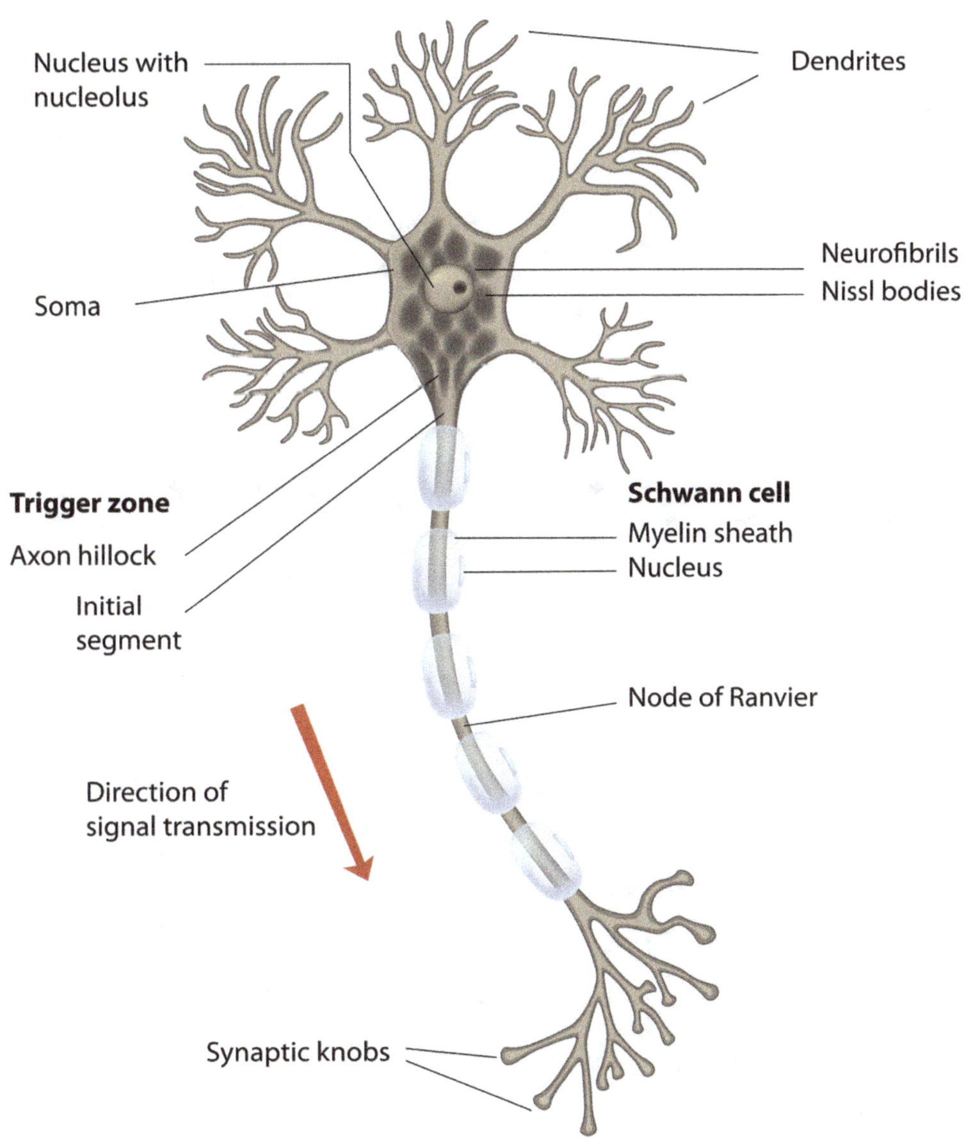

Reproductive System

STRUCTURE OF IN OVARY

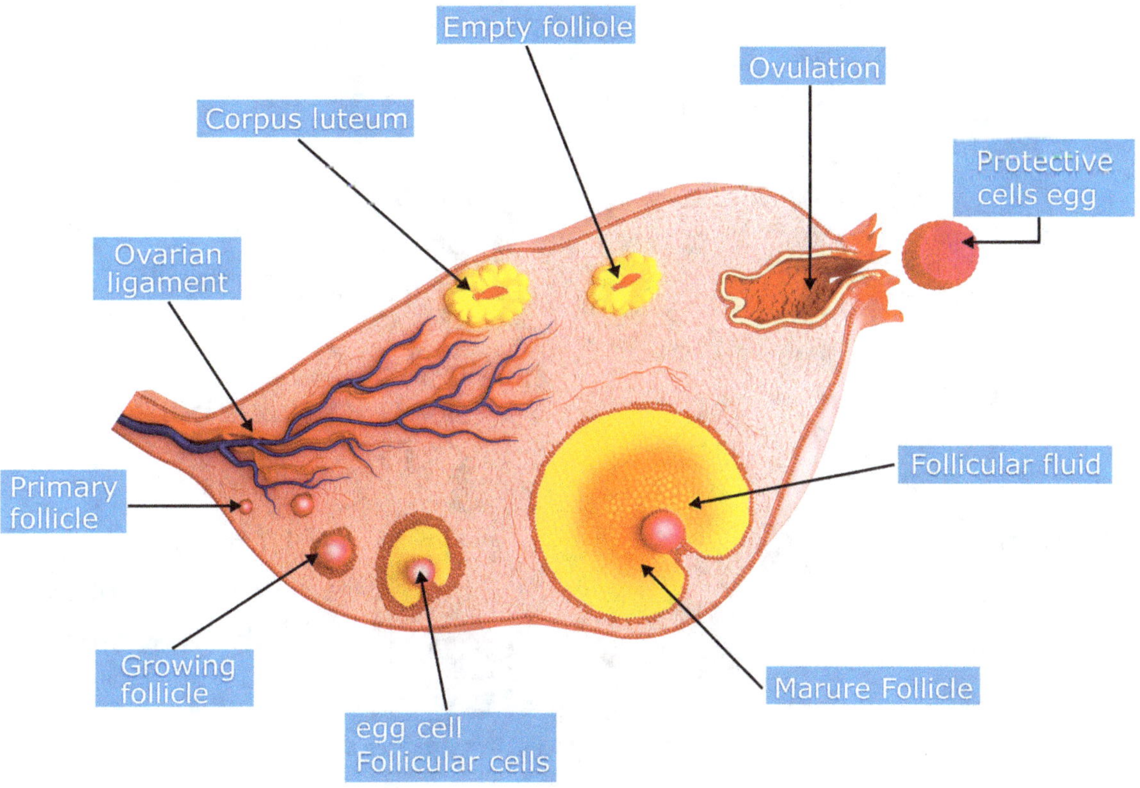

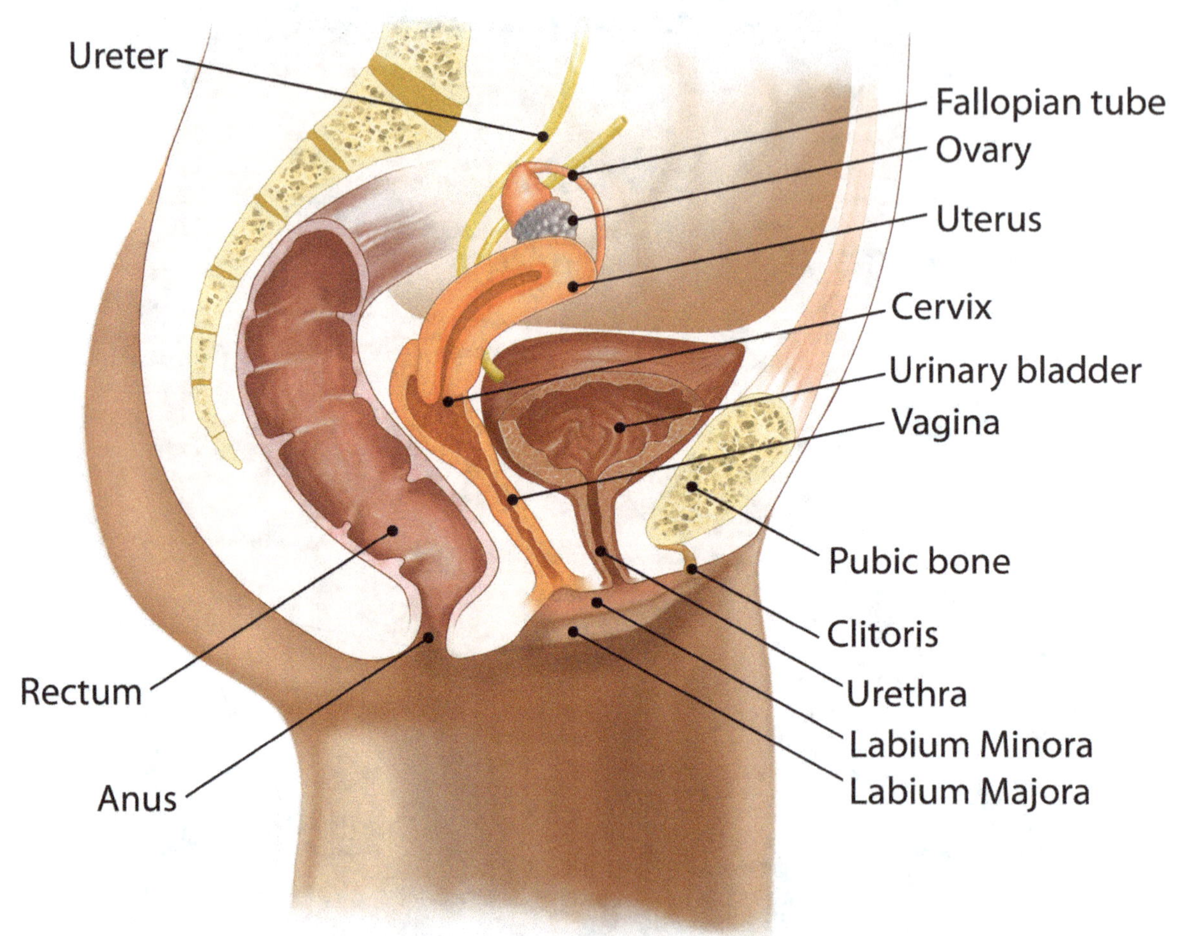
Ureter
Fallopian tube
Ovary
Uterus
Cervix
Urinary bladder
Vagina
Pubic bone
Clitoris
Urethra
Labium Minora
Labium Majora
Rectum
Anus

REPRODUCTIVE

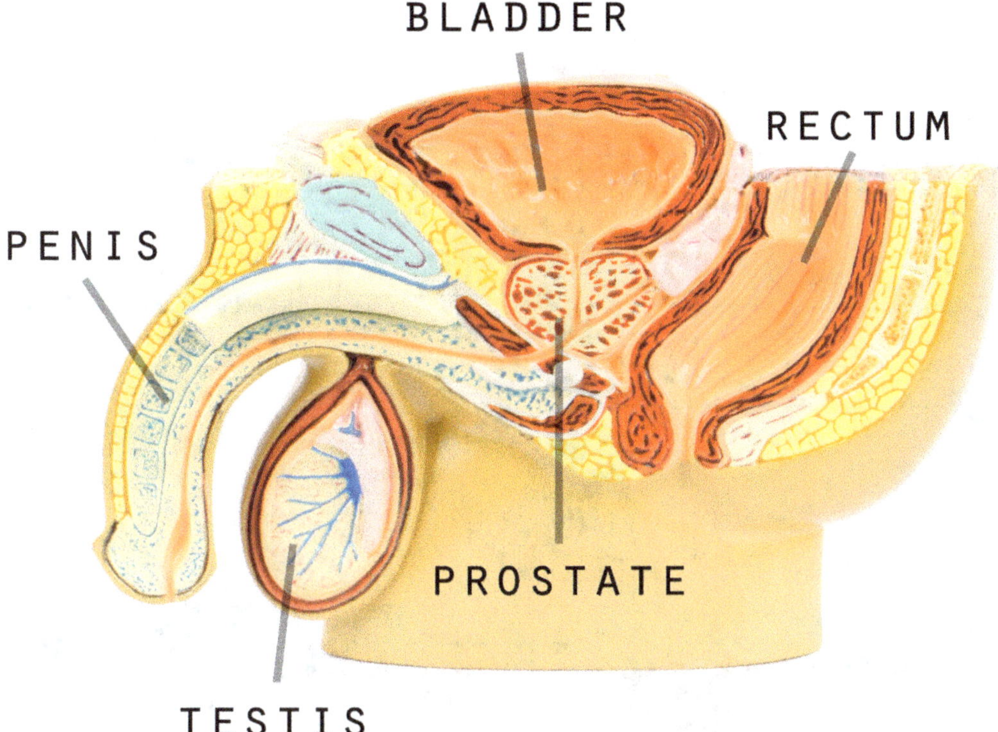

SCROTAL ANATOMY

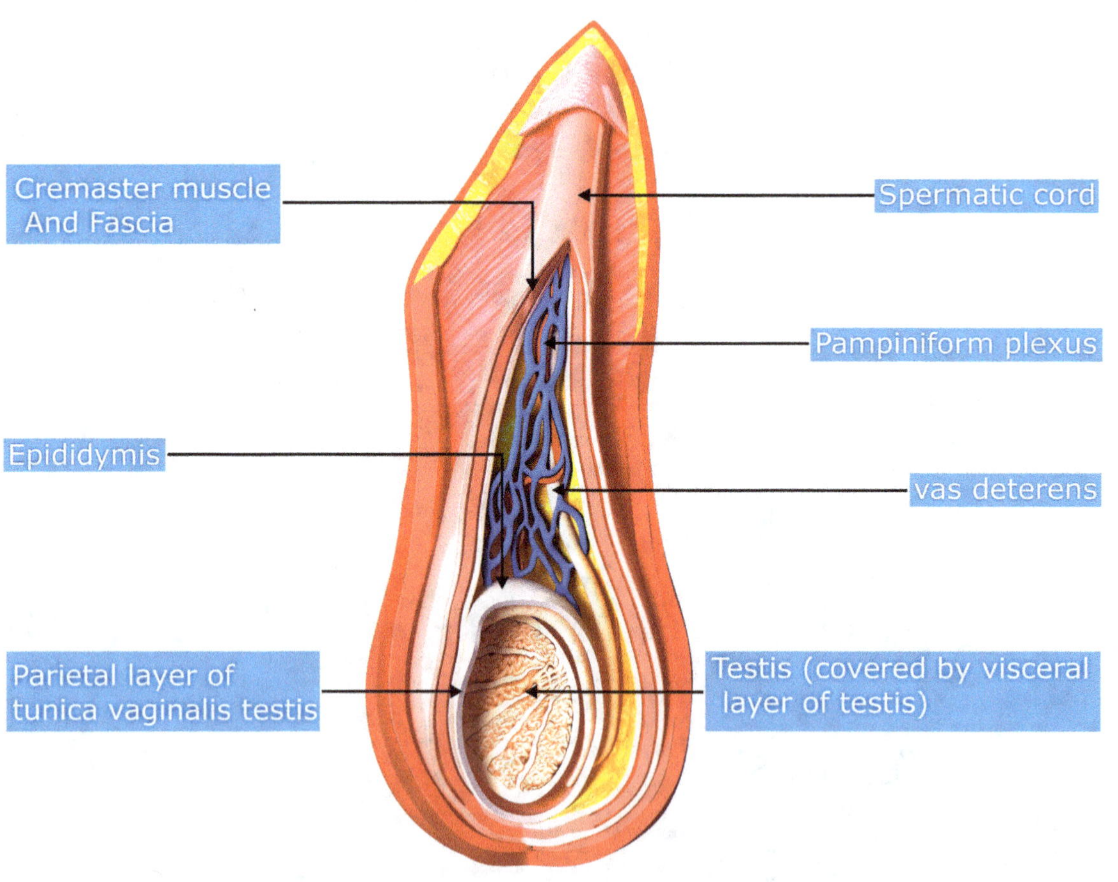

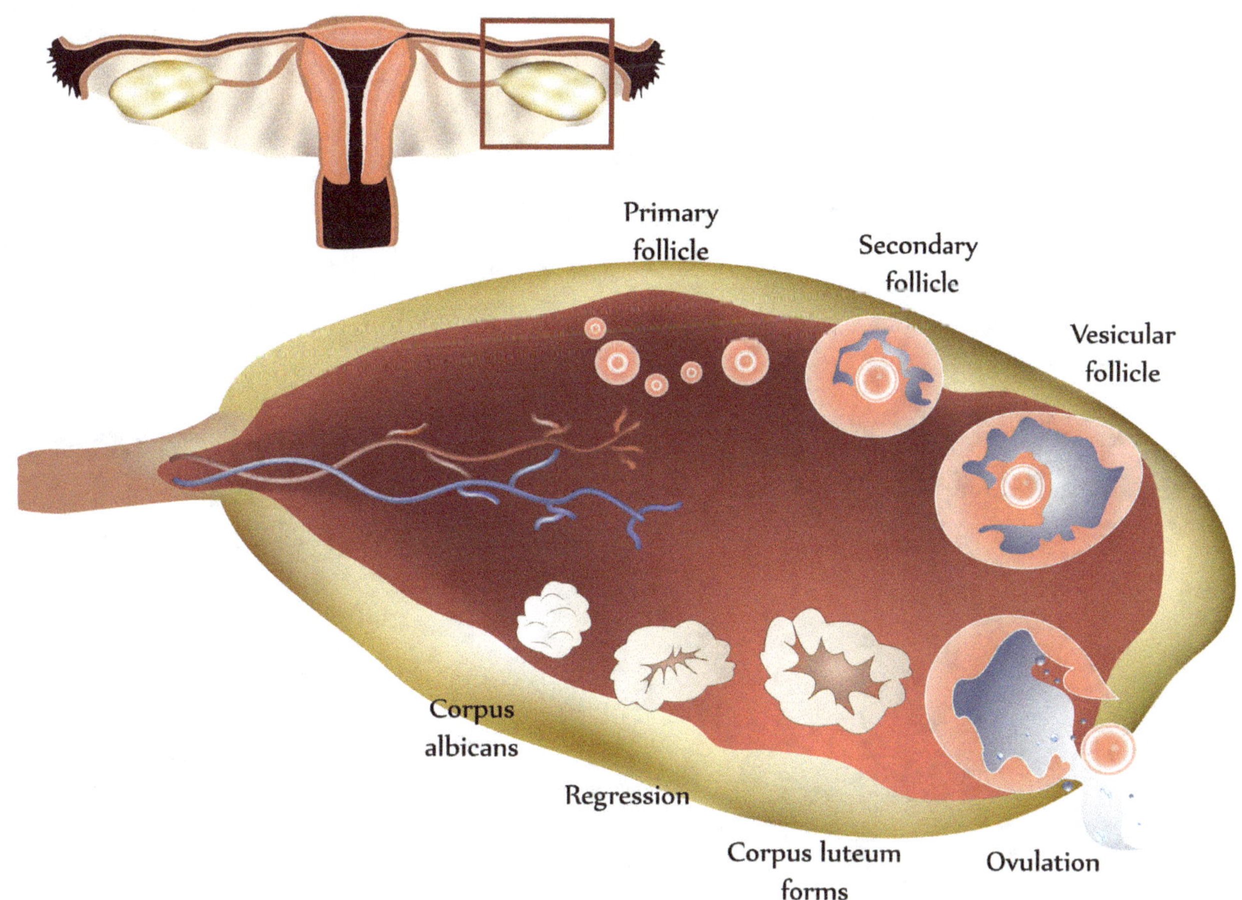
Primary
follicle
Secondary
follicle
Vesicular
follicle
Corpus
albicans
Regression
Corpus luteum
forms
Ovulation

Respiratory System

The Respiratory System

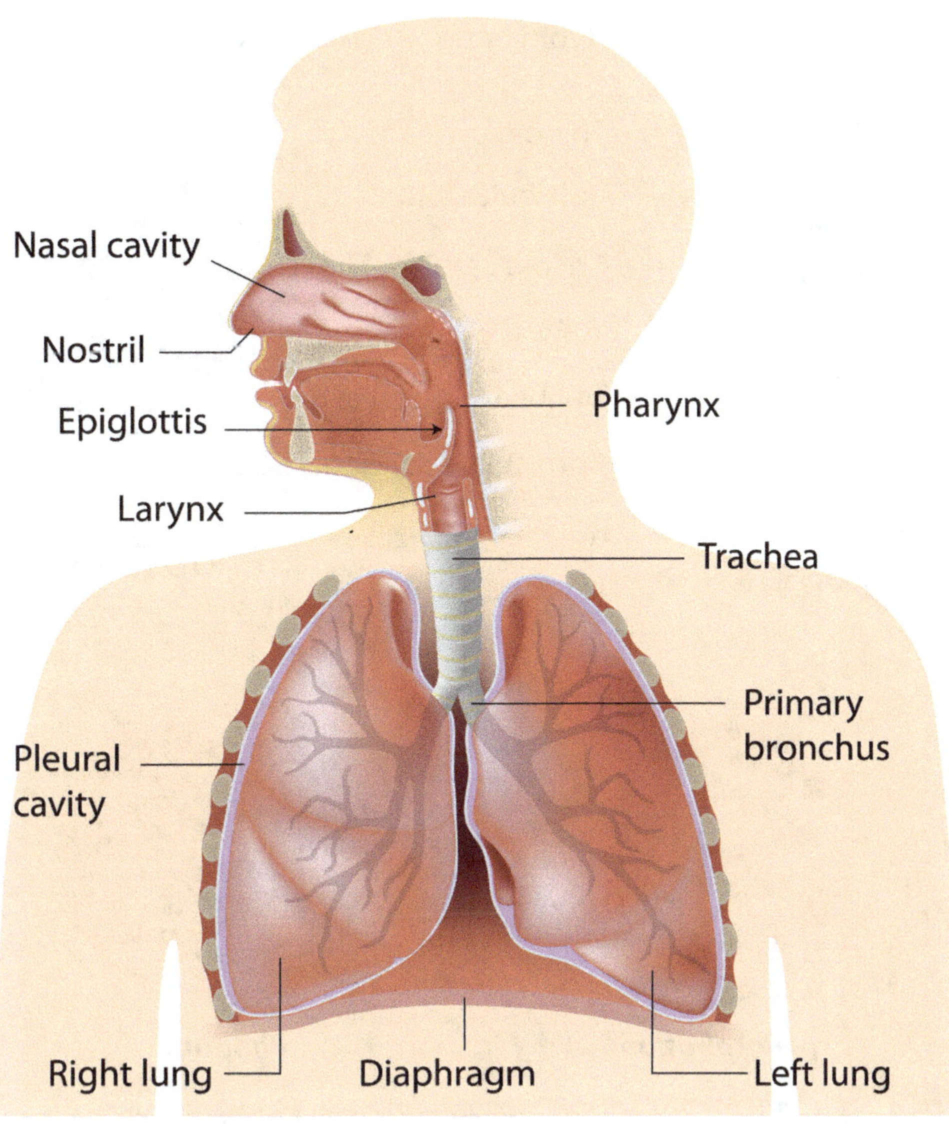

RESPIRATORY

The Larynx

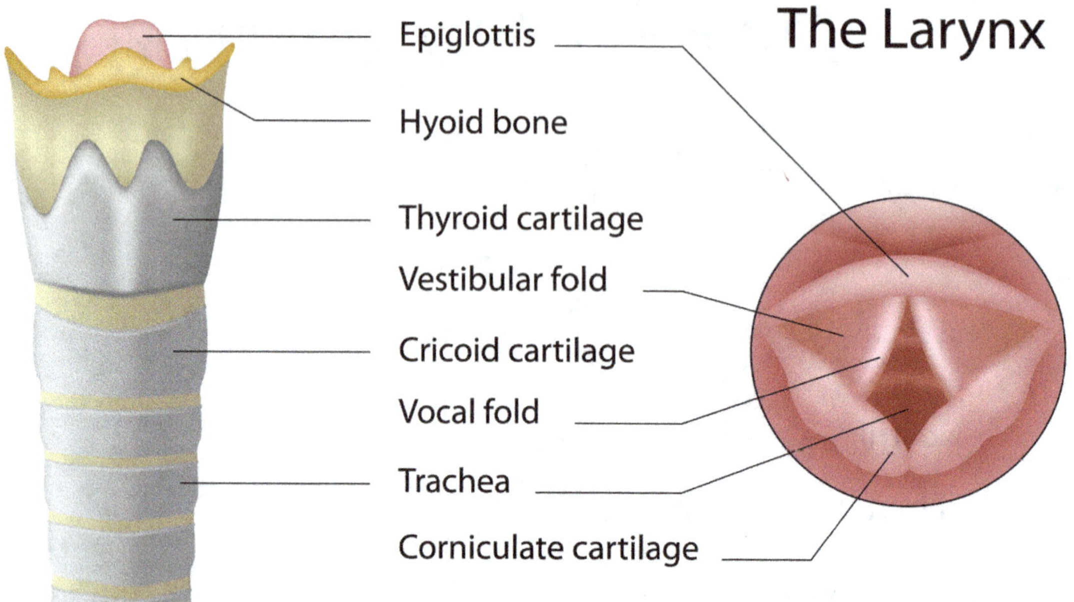

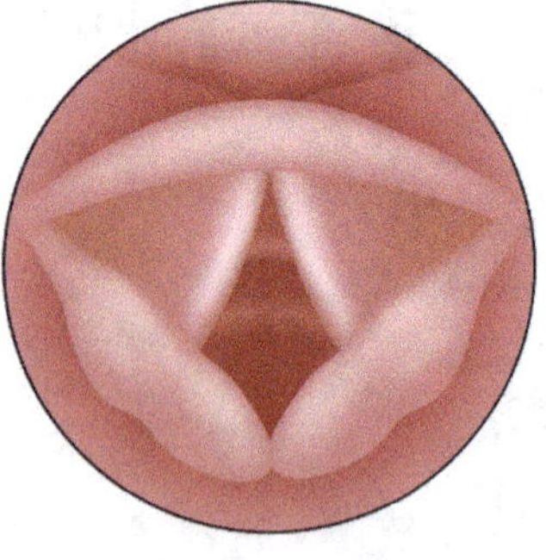

Respiration

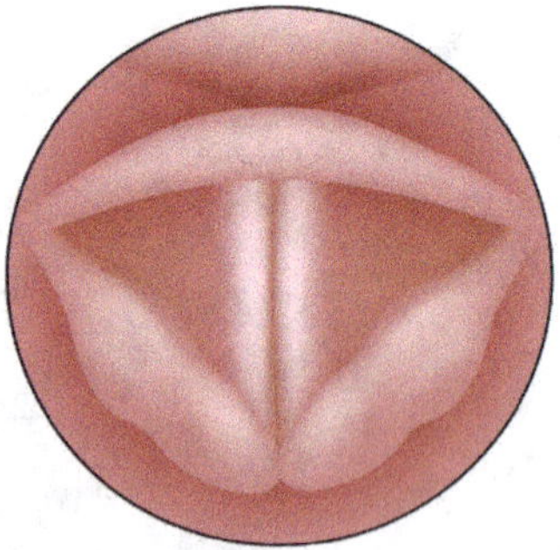

Phonation

Human Lung Anatomy and Function

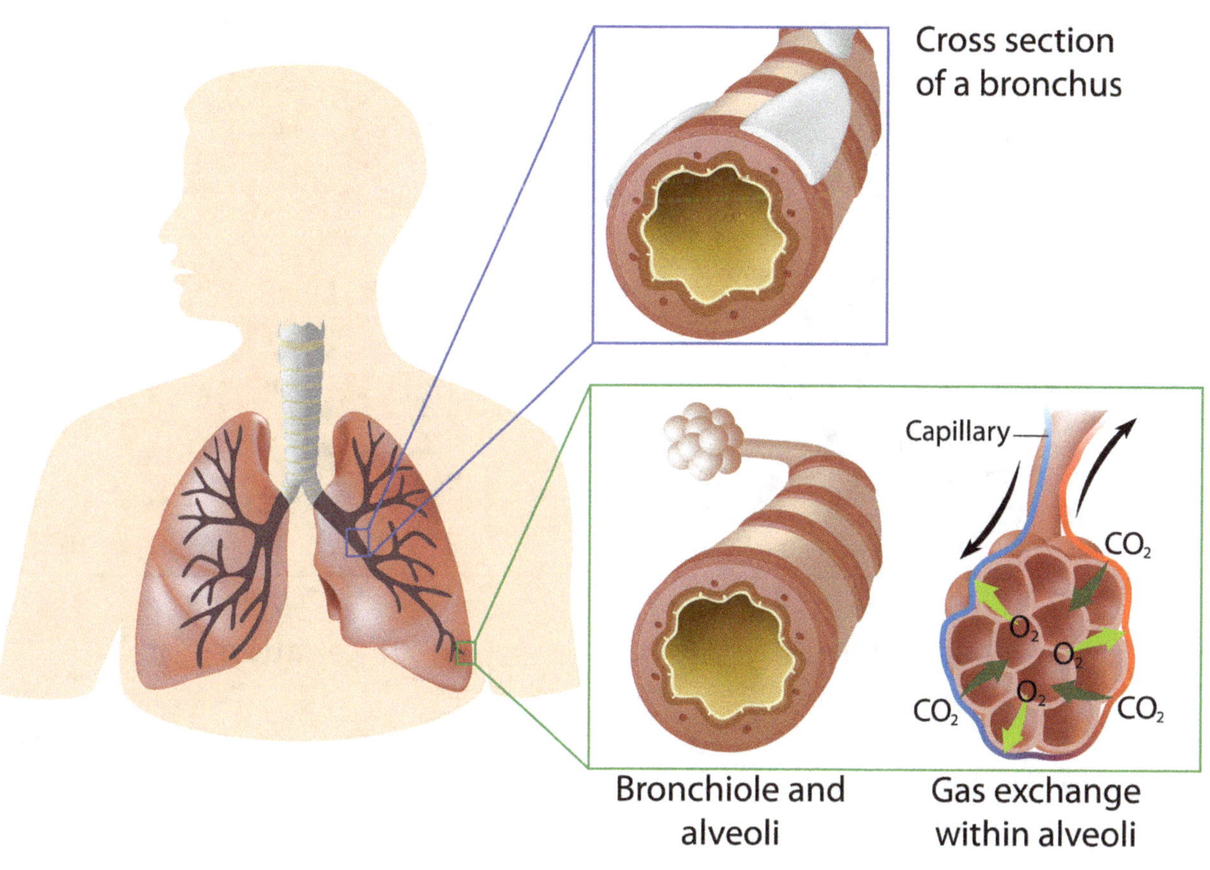

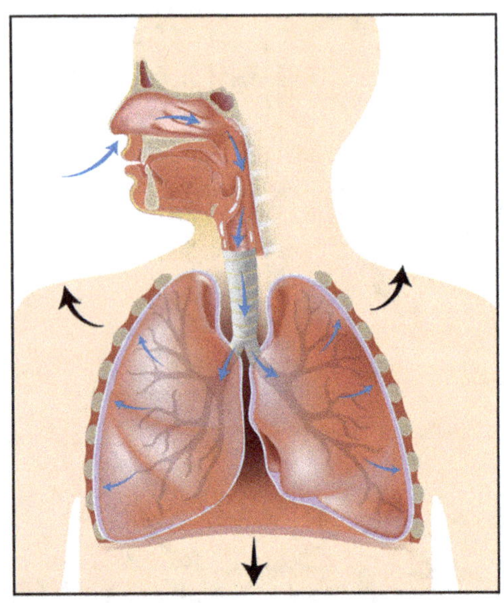

Inspiration

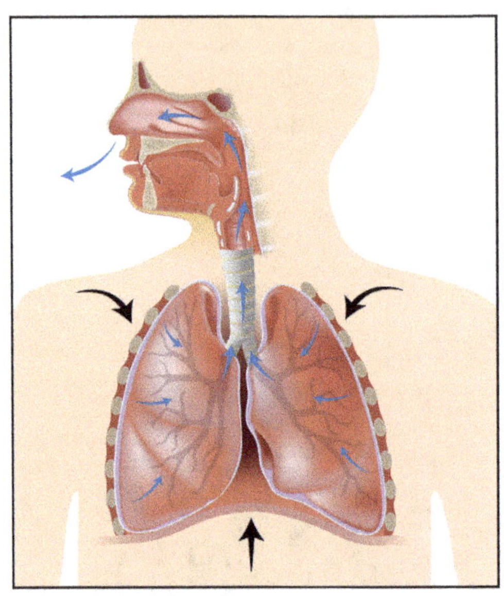

Expiration

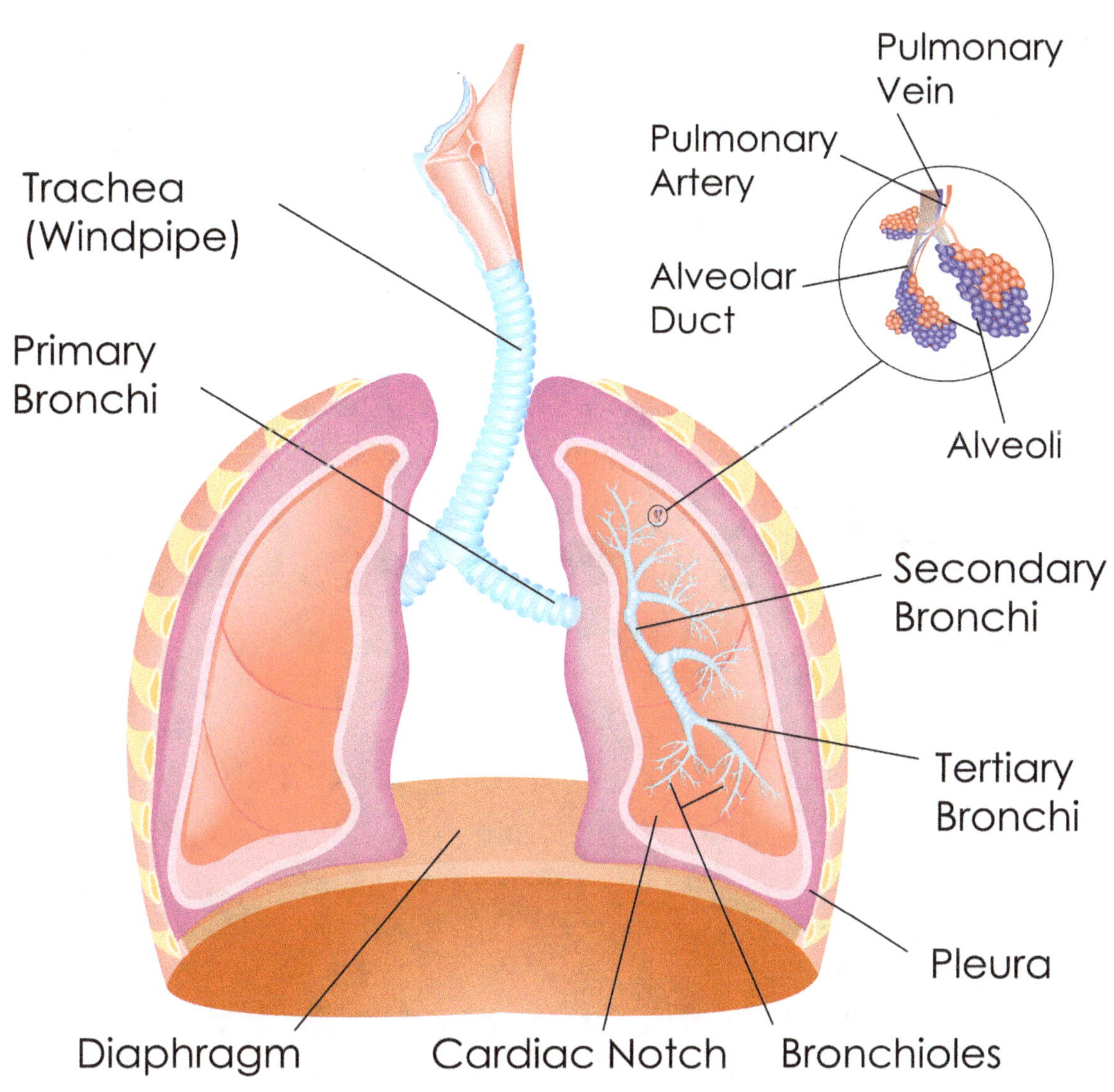
Trachea
(Windpipe)
Primary
Bronchi
Pulmonary
Vein
Pulmonary
Artery
Alveolar
Duct
Alveoli
Secondary
Bronchi
Tertiary
Bronchi
Pleura
Diaphragm
Cardiac Notch
Bronchioles

Skeletal System

BONE ANATOMY

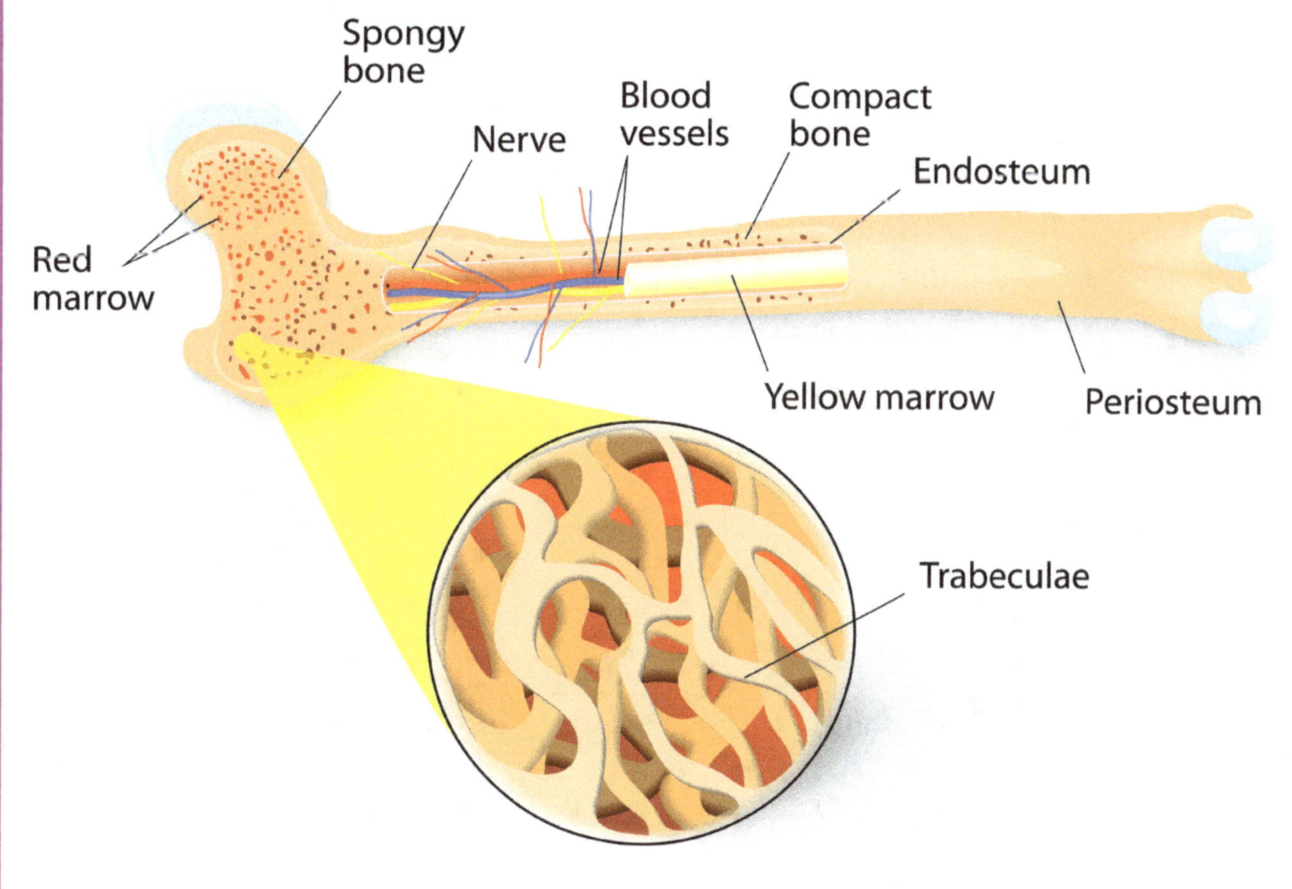

SKELETAL

Humerus
Medial epicondyle
Trochlea
Ulna
Head of radius
Radius
Olecranon
Coronoid process
Semilunar notch

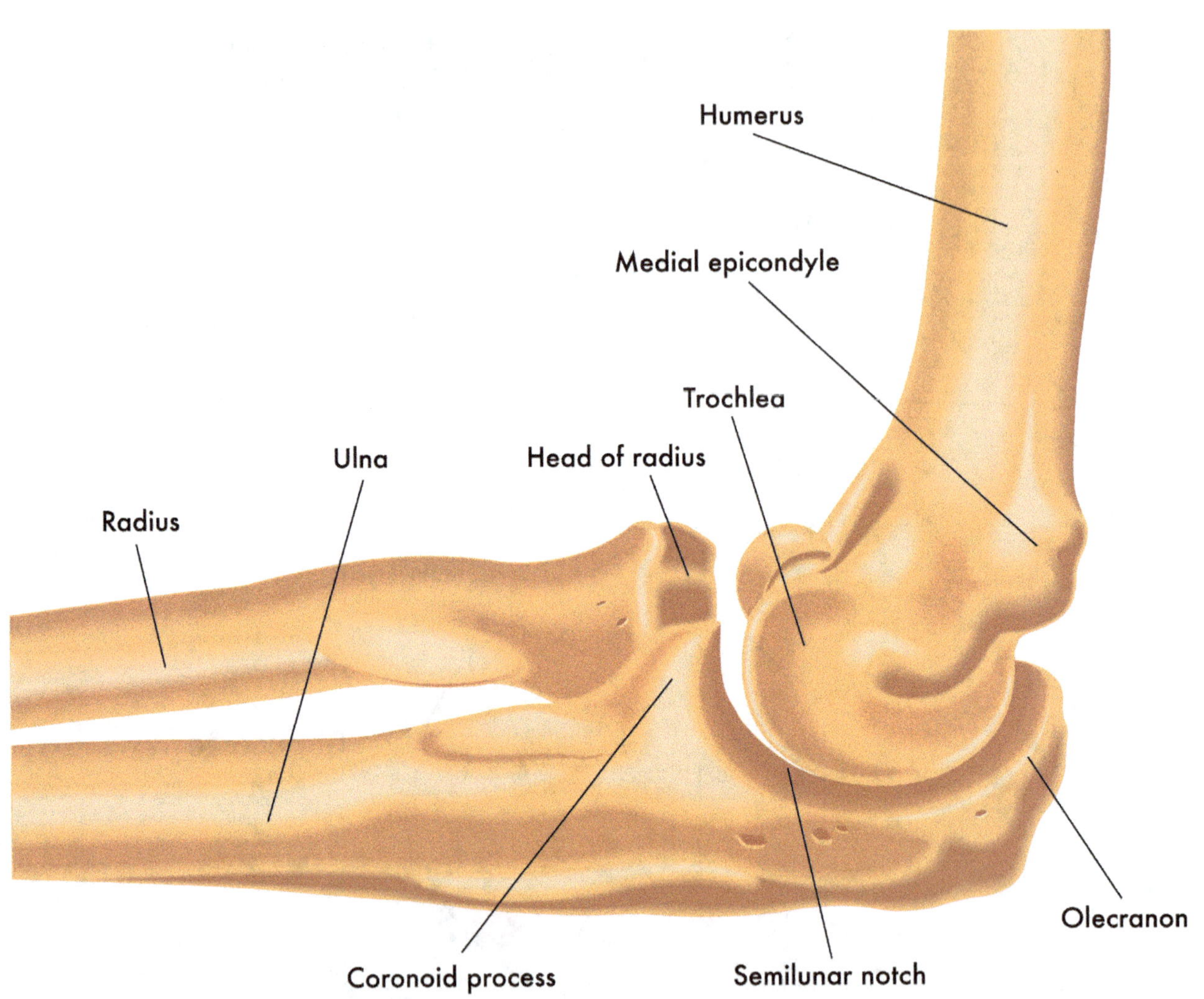

TIBIA AND FIBULA IN SECTION

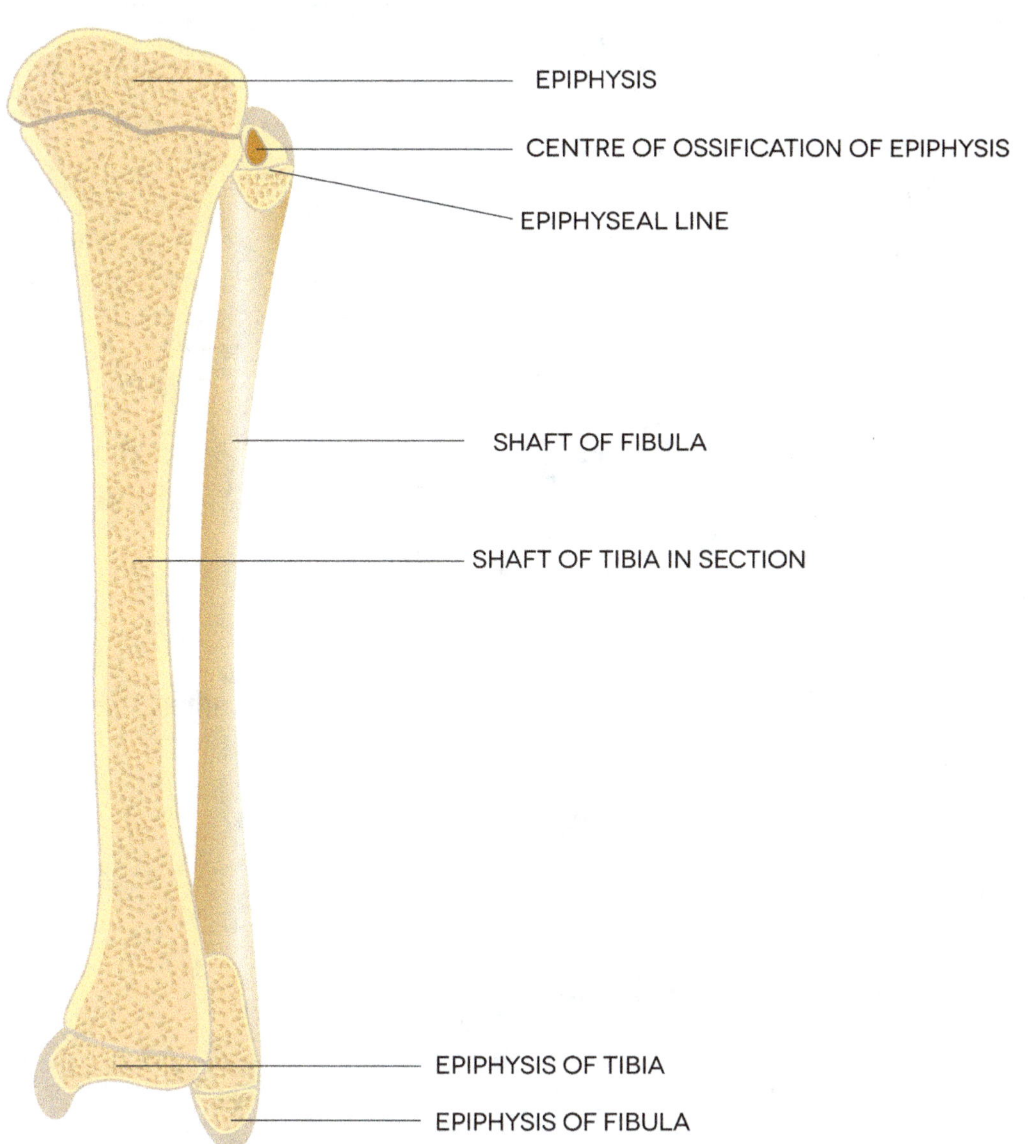

SKELETAL

Acromioclavicular joint
Clavicle
Glenohumeral joint
Scapula
Humerus
Scapulothoracic joint

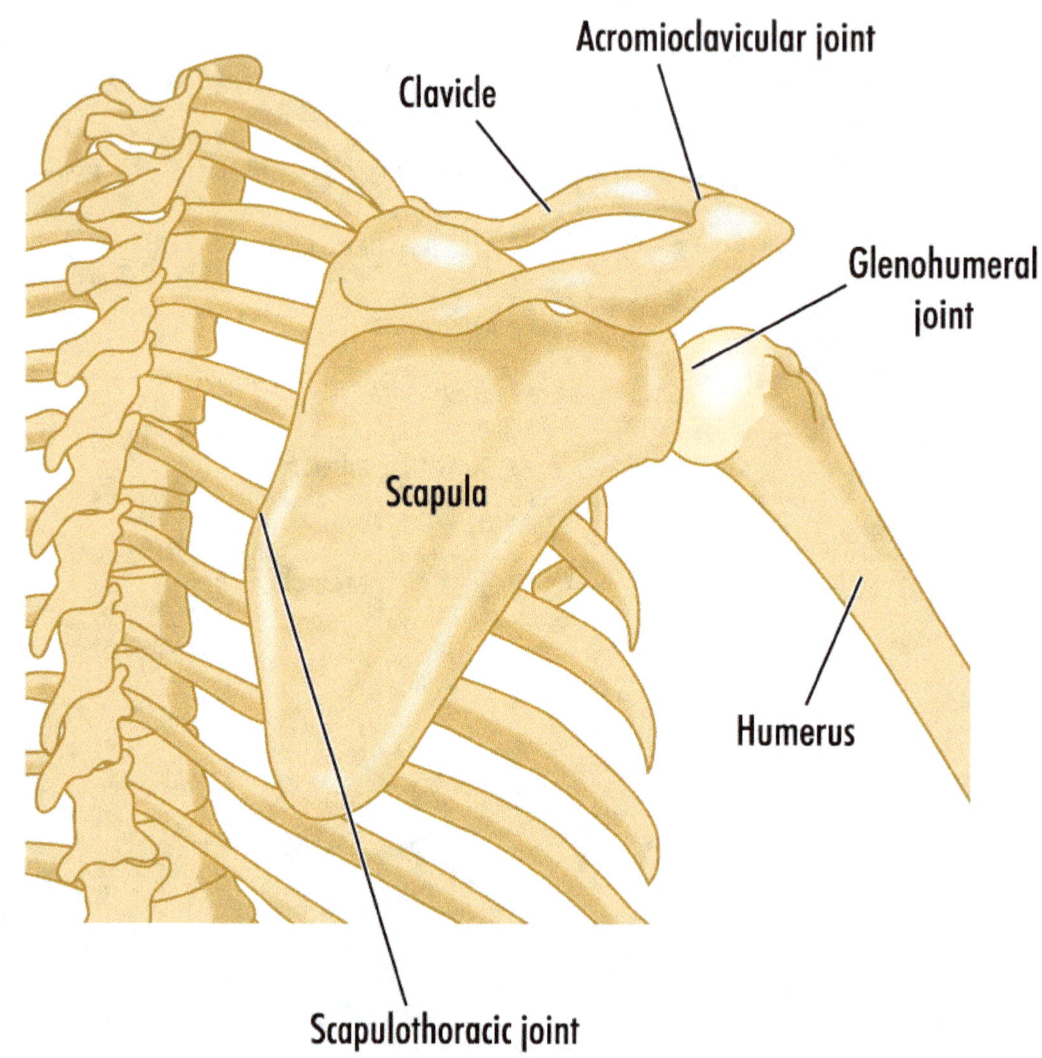

BONES OF THE UPPER EXTREMITY

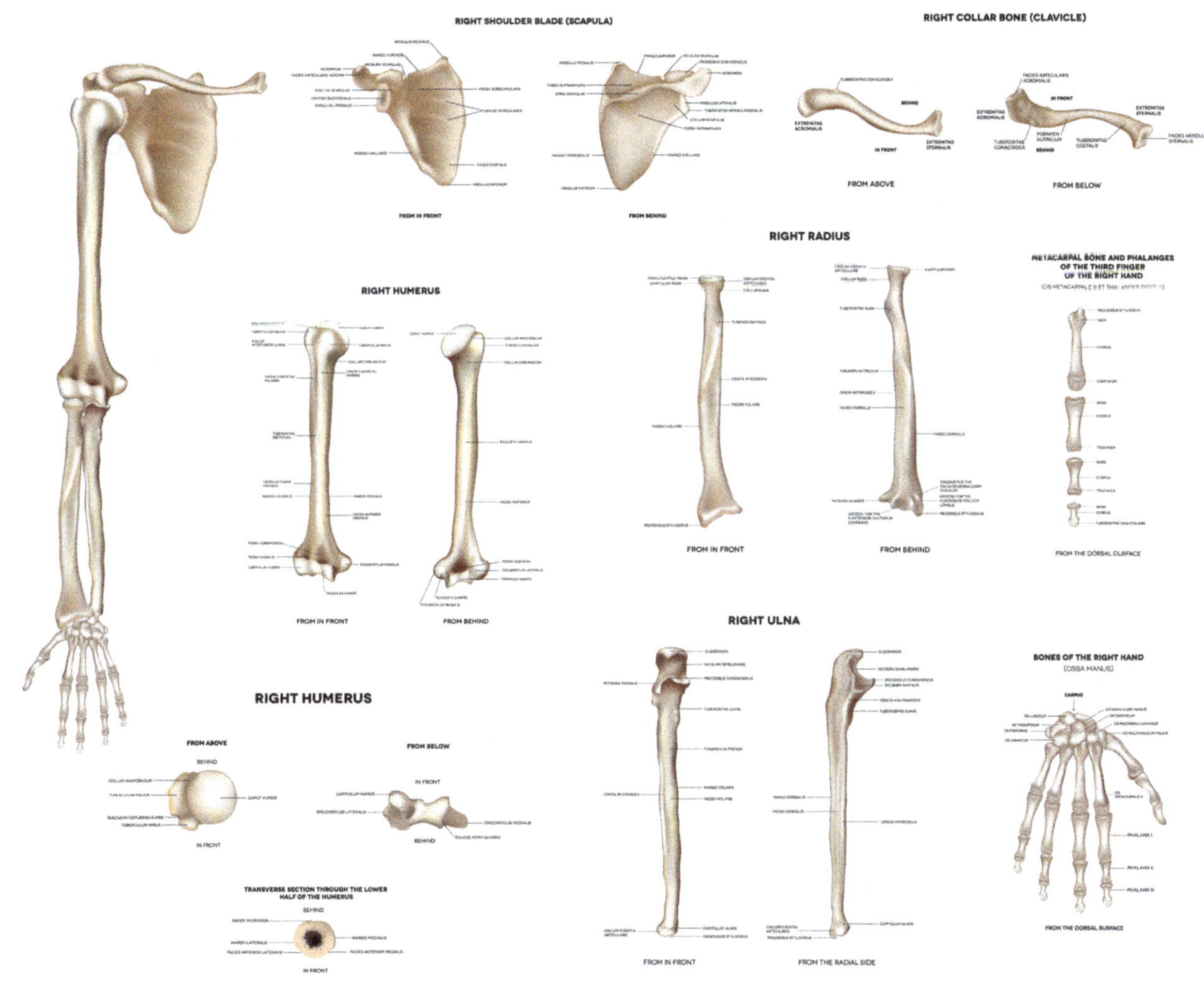

www.ingramcontent.com/pod-product-compliance
Lightning Source LLC
LaVergne TN
LVHW060508170826
845677LV00026B/1669
9798869456892